WITHDRAWN

MAR 14 2011

P9-DYE-208

family
FUN NIGHT!

by Cynthia L. Copeland

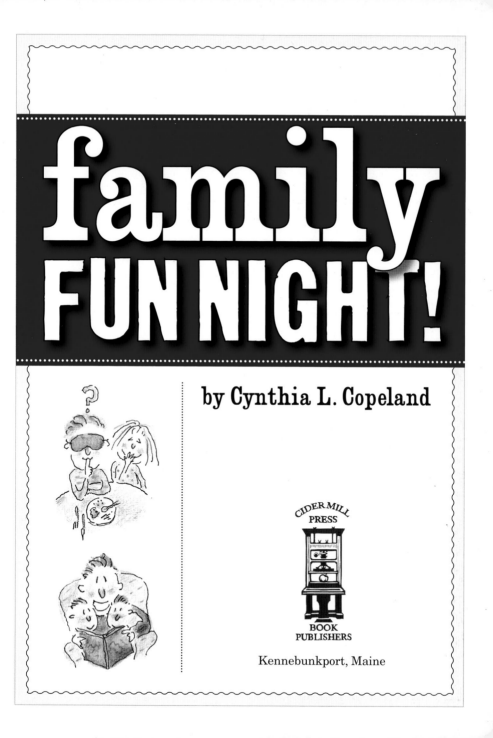

CIDER MILL
PRESS

BOOK
PUBLISHERS

Kennebunkport, Maine

13-Digit: 978-1-60433-094-6
10-Digit: 1-60433-094-5

This book may be ordered by mail from the publisher. Please include $2.50 for postage and handling. Please support your local bookseller first!

Books published by Cider Mill Press Book Publishers are available at special discounts for bulk purchases in the United States by corporations, institutions, and other organizations. For more information, please contact the publisher.

Cider Mill Press Book Publishers
"Where good books are ready for press"
12 Port Farm Road, Kennebunkport, Maine 04046

Visit us on the Web! www.cidermillpress.com

Design by Jessica Disbrow Talley
All illustrations courtesy of Cynthia L. Copeland

Printed in China

3 4 5 6 7 8 9 0

dedication

For my dad, who always puts family first

acknowledgements

This book could not have been completed without the dedication of my wonderful editor, Alexandra Lewis. Her suggestions, research assistance, and creative guidance were crucial throughout the writing process.

Many thanks, also, to my designer, Jessica Disbrow Talley, whose imaginative ideas and positive attitude make her a great partner in any project.

table of contents

SECTION ONE
THE BASICS

CHAPTER 1
why family fun night? 11

CHAPTER 2
getting everyone on board 15

CHAPTER 3
house rules 23

CHAPTER 4
sportsmanship 29

CHAPTER 5
activities for all ages 35

CHAPTER 6
treats for family fun night 41

SECTION 2
THE ACTIVITIES

CHAPTER 7
traditional board game night 49

CHAPTER 8
a charitable family fun night 75

CHAPTER 9
movie night 87

CHAPTER 10
family fun night picnic 111

CHAPTER 11
video game night 131

CHAPTER 12
ideas for last minute family fun nights 151

CHAPTER 13
read-aloud family fun night 163

CHAPTER 14
ideas for thrifty family fun nights 185

CHAPTER 15
card sharks night 199

CHAPTER 16
ideas for a family talent show night 229

CHAPTER 17
family scavenger hunt night 239

CHAPTER 18
family memories night 259

introduction

You may think it's the weeklong trip to Disneyland that your kids will remember, but it's more likely that they will recall the demented chicken that Dad drew during an all-play turn in Pictionary or the fact that Mom couldn't carry a tune in Rock Band. We remember the silly bonding moments, the times we felt a real connection as a family, the laughter. It doesn't matter whether your family likes to play Monopoly or musical instruments, make pizza or photo placemats. What matters is that your family establishes a regular time to have fun, enjoy one another's company, and create lasting memories. I'm hopeful that the ideas in this book will encourage your family to start your own unique Family Fun Night tradition.

The book is divided into two sections. The first offers general information about game nights: ways to engage the kids, age-appropriate activities, and rules to make things run more smoothly. The second details specific game nights your family might enjoy. You can follow one plan from start to finish, or you can browse through and choose bits and pieces from each game night, mixing and matching to suit your family's needs. Everything, including suggestions for meals or snacks, is included for each special night.

Sidebars include tips to enhance the fun, personal stories to inspire families, and a little history lesson now and then.

I hope you'll have a wonderful time making family memories!

Cindy

CHAPTER ONE

why family fun night?

Despite surveys proclaiming that families value time together more than anything else, busy schedules on the part of both parents and kids have often gotten in the way. One extensive survey found that from 1981 to 1997, household conversations dropped by 100 percent! This means that the average family reported no time during the week when family members sat down just to chat. The number of families that had dinner together on a regular basis dropped by one-third during that same period. Sadly, a family's "together" time meant a few kids lounging in front of the TV while someone else played on the computer and another chatted with a friend on the phone.

TIDBIT: A December 2005 Gallup poll asked people to name their favorite way to spend an evening. The most popular response? Staying home with the family (32%), which beat out watching television and reading, numbers two and three.

But in the twenty-first century, things are changing. Due in part to a significant economic shift, family values and family activities are beginning to coincide. Staying in has become the new going out, with "cocooning" more appealing to many families as budgets tighten and money allocated for entertainment shrinks. In greater numbers, multiple generations are living together under one roof, meaning that there are more people in a household who can interact with one another. As a result of these shifts, board game sales have soared recently. Families are rediscovering the simpler pleasures of each other's company.

TIDBIT: The folks in Ridgewood, NJ inspired other communities nationwide when they declared March 26, 2002 "Family Night." Teachers were asked not to assign homework, coaches were expected to cancel practices and games, school performances were moved to different days—even town and school meetings were postponed. Watching television was forbidden. A follow-up survey found that most Ridgewood families appreciated the evening that was devoted to family bonding.

It's true that many things continue to compete for our attention, even at home: video and computer games, homework, texting friends, or checking social networking sites. Teenagers, especially, will always be drawn to their peers; it's a natural and necessary part of growing up. But family members are starting to have a greater appreciation for one another, establishing new traditions centered around old-fashioned family values.

 # MY STORY

"I find that we learn a lot more about our kids' lives during game night than at any other time. Their defenses are down and they tend to chat about things that they would normally not share with us. Conversation is easier than when we're quizzing them about their day-to-day activities."

-Lakisha, mother of three

CHAPTER TWO

getting everyone on board

Most children are excited about the idea of family night. For a six-year-old, an evening spent playing cards with Mom and Dad is about as good as it gets! Once you establish the tradition, they will be counting down to the next Family Fun Night.

 ## MY STORY

"Initially, we had trouble getting everyone together. We were too hung up on the idea of a Friday or Saturday night. When we discovered that late afternoon on Sunday seemed to be a more convenient time for everyone, we were able to start a real tradition."

-Nancy, mother of two

If they seem less than enthusiastic, take them to the store and let them select a new board game. Or begin with a movie night (see Chapter 9) and allow your most reluctant child to choose the film.

It will take a while for everyone to get used to the idea of regular time away from video games and the computer. Your attitude is contagious, though, and as long as you act excited (and not stressed out) about the idea, your kids will follow your lead. You're not trying to recreate a three-ring circus or amusement park experience, just going for some fun and relaxation with the people who mean the most to you.

 # MY STORY

"The trick is to focus on the fun of family night, not make it one more thing on the to-do list."

-Sherry, mother of three

• • • • • •

"My seven-year-old idolizes a girl in her class named Sarah whose mother I know well. I asked my friend if we could borrow one of Sarah's favorite board games for our first family night and my daughter couldn't wait to learn how to play!"

-Dana, mother of one

7 WAYS
to excite kids
about family night

1. Use sticky notes to remind everyone about the fun evening you have planned: Come up with clever phrases that will entice them and affix the notes to bathroom mirrors, computer screens, and dinner plates.

2. Save mementos from activities you've done together in the past (like a funny sketch from Pictionary) and hang them in prominent places with a note: "Who remembers this 'dog' that looks just like a horse?"

3. If your kids enjoy competition, set up Family Fun Night as a series of rounds in a tournament that will lead to a championship round.

4. Reward winners with tickets that can be exchanged for small prizes. Establish a rule that before the "prize center" opens for business, every child must have tickets to redeem.

5. Alter games to suit your family's interests. If your daughter loves horses, buy her a small horse that is her own special token for Monopoly.

6. Get together with another family whose kids are favorites of your children.

7. Allow anxious children to watch as the rest of the family plays. It won't be long before they are begging to be included.

TIP: Prizes don't have to cost a thing! How about offering up an extra half hour of TV on a Sunday morning, an extra half hour added to bedtime, a bonus bedtime story, or the privilege of riding in the front seat of the car for a whole week?

If you have a stepfamily, it can be a challenge to line up everyone's schedules because often there isn't daily communication. One way to ensure that everyone will be together is to plan family nights for weekends when you take the whole crew out of town. Removing kids from their peer groups will allow them to connect with the family. If staying in a hotel is not an option, trade houses with an out-of-town family or stay with friends or relatives.

 # MY STORY

"We had the best family nights when we stayed in my parents' guest house. There was no TV, no computer, nothing but a cabinet full of games, cards, and books. No one even knew the phone number, so the phone never rang! We all felt relaxed and free to enjoy each other's company."

-Cathy, mother of three, stepmother of three

Pre-teens and teens can be harder to get on board than younger kids. Despite the fact that in a recent YMCA poll, 21 percent of teens listed "not having enough time together with parents" as their most significant concern, it's natural for them to resist spending a Friday or Saturday night at home. Ignore their grumbling! You can allow reluctant participants to invite a friend or start the tradition with a video game night (see Chapter 11) if they'll agree to play a classic board game the next time the family gets together. Or propose a game that they are likely to want to learn how to play, like poker. Use real poker chips (www.gamedaze.com) so they'll feel like they're part of an adult game.

TIDBIT: Don't assume that all boys would rather be out on the town! A 2001 Gallup Youth Survey that asked girls and boys how they would prefer to spend an evening found that more girls than boys—42 percent to 30 percent—said that they would prefer to spend an evening with their friends. Boys were more likely than girls to say they didn't mind hanging at home!

 # MY STORY

"We couldn't get our middle schoolers interested in family night until one summer evening when we pulled them into a game of flashlight tag. They loved it! We have expanded our repertoire to include laser tag with a set of laser guns and vests that I bought over the Internet."

-Becky, mother of three

TIP: Teens will do just about anything—even homework– if they can listen to their favorite music. Perhaps for the first family get-together, you can allow them to hook their iPods to speakers and select the background music. One parent said that her teens liked rap music (which she couldn't tolerate) so they compromised on Spanish rap, which had the beat her kids liked but no one was offended because they didn't understand the lyrics!

Lure teens with rewards they will appreciate: The night's grand prize can be an extra hour added to a Saturday night curfew, use of the car keys for a night, first rights to the bathroom every morning for a week, a video game party with friends or a sleepover.

Once you have established a consistent family night, most teens won't require bribes. But don't feel guilty about doing what you need to at first so that they'll stay connected to family. They won't realize (until they're a little older) that the real reward of taking part in family night is the bond they strengthen with you and with their siblings and the great memories they'll have.

 # MY STORY

"We had trouble getting our teenage sons interested in game night. Finally we bought a dartboard and darts and said that we were having a tournament. They loved the idea! It's just adult enough to appeal to them."

-Mike, father of two

• • • • • •

"[My favorite way to spend an evening is] at home with my family. I like to cook and I help my parents prepare the meals for all six of us. I play lots of video games with my brothers, but my favorite is when we play board games with all of us, including my parents. We like to watch movies together on TV. We do lots of talking and laughing in the evenings when we are all together."

-Respondent to a 2003 Gallup poll asking teens how they prefer to spend an evening, quoted from gallup.com

CHAPTER THREE

house rules

You'll want to establish some general rules for Family Fun Night to prevent arguments and avoid confusion. Basically, the rules are intended to make sure that everyone in the family attends cheerfully, that there are no distractions, and that everyone understands how each game is played.

To start, how will you determine what each week's activity will be? Maybe you'll want to take turns choosing. This works best if children select from a master list of games and activities (rather than from their vast imaginations). If you elect to do this, the person who makes the selection can be in charge of setting up the game or activity, explaining the rules, and cleaning up. Another option—one with an element of surprise—is to pull ideas written on slips of paper from a Family Fun Night jar. Creative folks can make their own game spinner with an arrow that will point to the chosen activity. Inevitably, some in the group will be happy with the choice and some won't be. But an important rule that you'll want to enforce from the start is that everyone will participate with a positive attitude and an open mind.

our family night rules

1. Once a night is chosen and agreed upon, everyone must keep it free for Family Fun Night.

2. At the end of each Family Fun Night, the date and activity of the next gathering will be set.

3. The phone will be on silent mode and the answering machine will be turned on for the evening.

4. No text messaging, cell phone communication, or fiddling with BlackBerries allowed.

5. The computer and TV will be turned off.

6. We will not talk about unpleasant news headlines, family problems, or anything likely to take the edge off of the fun. If there is an elephant-in-the-room topic, we will spend five minutes on it, then move on.

7. Here's how we will handle clean-up: _____

_____

8. _____

_____

rules to play by

For Family Fun Night to run smoothly, the rules of each activity need to be articulated and understood by everyone. It doesn't matter whether you follow the rules as they are written for an individual game or you decide to make up your own, they just need to be agreed upon by all players.

TIP: If everyone agrees, you can have special rules for the younger kids in the family. For a game of volleyball, for instance, you can allow kids under five to pick up the ball and throw it over the net.

If you choose to develop your own rules, you'll need to write them down. You may want to start a journal in which you write down the rules you've agreed upon for various games. That way, you can look them up in the event of a disagreement. Children must also understand the importance of everyone following the same rules. When the rules have been established, a parent can read them aloud, and then the family can play one round as a practice round to be sure everyone understands.

TIP: Agree as a family how you will decide who goes first in a board game, who is "it" in an outdoor game of tag, or who is the leader in a game like Simon Says. Here are a few ideas:

1. Draw straws (the short straw wins)

2. Pick numbers from one to ten and see whose number is closest to the number Mom's thinking of

3. Roll dice to see who gets the highest number

4. Flip a coin (for two kids)

5. Play rock/paper/scissors (for two kids)

If it's necessary to choose teams, a parent may want to make the assignments so that the sides are evenly matched. This doesn't mean that the numbers need to be even: You can pit the family's chess champ against the rest of the group. Even if teams aren't required, they can be helpful when there is a significant age spread. A board game like Monopoly can be played as a team game. For games involving more luck than skill, names can be drawn from a hat. In games of chance, the kids may get a kick out of teaming up against the parents. If it seems like that would work out, let them go for it!

Although a team can work with members simply rotating turns and decision-making, in the case of a mixed age team, it's probably best to choose a team leader who, after consulting with the other members, will make the final decision on a move or a play.

TIP: Come up with acceptable ways to resolve disagreements that may arise during a game. You may want to take one of these suggestions:

1. For every game, appoint a judge who will make a decision if there is a stalemate (allow two minutes for the disputing parties to work it out themselves before the judge gets involved)

2. Flip a coin

3. Re-play the round in question

Finally, you'll need to decide how to handle cheating. What should the consequences be? It's less emotional if the ground rules are established before the situation arises. You might have the person who cheated miss the next turn or lose a certain number of points. It's trickier if a player is accused of cheating and vehemently denies it. If there is no consensus that cheating occurred, you may simply have to continue the game, with a general reminder that a victory based on cheating is no victory at all.

sportsmanship

Family Fun Night offers lots of opportunities to teach important lessons about winning and losing gracefully, taking turns, following rules, and using good manners. Teaching and practicing these skills happen naturally within the context of playing games.

TIDBIT: Should parents let kids win? Most parents and child-rearing experts agree that parents shouldn't play a game poorly in order to let a child win. There is not much to be gained by doing that. The best idea is to change the rules so that the playing field is even: Start the child off with extra letters in Scrabble or extra points in badminton. If the age spread is very wide, create even teams. That way, both parents and kids can try their hardest and enjoy the game.

It can be difficult to convey the message to our kids that winning isn't everything. Parents are up against powerful media messages about the value of winning (think about the slogan from an ad that ran during the Atlanta Olympics: "You don't win silver; you lose gold"). As adults, we know the truth behind the familiar adage stressing "how you play the game," but that can be a tricky concept for little folks to embrace. It's important, though, to make it clear from the start that boastful winners and sore losers are not acceptable on game night.

TIP: You know your kids best. If they thrive on healthy competition and consistently exhibit good sportsmanship, make a colorful poster with scores recorded each week. If competition creates bad feelings or too much anxiety, just play for fun and don't keep score.

A game winner can certainly celebrate, but parents might need to remind him to do so without making the other players feel inferior. After all, no one wins every game, and it's likely that the winner of this game won't be the winner of the next. Establish a tradition around winning that recognizes and rewards the victory, but contains it. Others might congratulate the winner with a high five, or allow the winner to go first in the next round, or choose the next game.

Those who don't win need to accept the outcome gracefully. Remind them to study the strategies used by the winners so that they can try them in the next round. It's been said many times that people learn more from failure than from success, so kids should regard a loss as an opportunity to improve their skills. Remind everyone that the real winners are those who have a great time, learn something new, realize the satisfaction of trying their hardest, and enjoy the time spent with family. No one's going to remember who won round four of Scrabble on the third Friday in March.

You can help your child respond appropriately throughout the night by employing a strategy that is based on his or her temperament. An emotional child must learn to compose and calm himself before reacting to a situation; you can tell him to count silently to 10 before responding or to notice clues about himself when he is getting upset so that he can avoid inappropriate behavior. Children who are perfectionists need to be reminded about all of the things they've accomplished, learned, and done correctly, not the ways in which they fell short. Kids who act out when things don't go their way need to be warned about the specific consequences of inappropriate behavior, such as sitting out during the next round due to a temper tantrum.

The most significant thing that parents can do is to model good behavior. Offer praise and encouragement to all players, and take winning and losing in stride. Show your kids that you can enjoy something (Guitar Hero, maybe?) without necessarily being great at it. Look for teachable moments throughout the course of the evening, and reinforce humility and empathy whenever possible.

the good sport contract

If you are coping with issues of poor sportsmanship, have everyone sign a Good Sport Contract. It could say something like:

I promise that I will do my best to be a good sport on Family Fun Nights. I will play fair and not cheat, I will not lose my temper, I will not criticize my teammates or blame them for a loss, I will lose gracefully, I will not brag about a win but I will always congratulate the winner, and I will accept the judge's final decision in the case of a disagreement.

Signed,

_____

_____

_____

_____

_____

_____

CHAPTER FIVE

activities
for all ages

It's important to choose activities that are appropriate for the ages of your kids. Most games have a recommended age range, which will help you decide. In addition, there are some general age-group guidelines that might prove useful when you are determining what might be the most fun for your family.

➡ THREE AND UNDER

For the littlest tykes, the best games are open-ended and can be adapted as play continues. You may find that you and your child establish your own rules rather than play by the rules that come with the game. Ideal games are ones where chance is a more significant factor than skill or physical ones with simple rules. Each game should be relatively short, allowing you to play several rounds or several different games in one night.

TIP: One way to include a young child in a Family Fun Night with older kids is to team her up with a parent or older sibling, or give her tasks such as rolling the dice, turning over a sand timer, or moving game pieces.

➡ FOUR- AND FIVE-YEAR-OLDS

This is a good time to begin playing games that require taking turns, sharing, and following simple rules. Activities involving fantasy, imagination, and creativity are especially popular with four- and five-year-olds.

Look for board games that don't require players to read, like Chutes and Ladders and Candyland. Clue Little Detective Game, in which players match colors rather than read words, is perfect for pre-readers and will prepare them for more advanced games of Clue. Don't Spill the Beans and Don't Break the Ice are also fun games intended for kids in this age group. If they want to play more adult games, simplify the rules and shorten the game so that they can be included.

 MY STORY

"I discovered that my five-year-old and I were more evenly matched in a game if the theme was something that really interested him. I bought two decks of cards with dinosaur pictures and facts, and we play Concentration with them. He is much more likely to remember where the other Parasaurolophus is than I am!"

-Michelle, mother of two

➡ SIX- TO NINE-YEAR-OLDS

Children six to nine are able to pay attention for longer stretches of time and will start to show an interest in more adult board games. They understand concept of teamwork and have a keen interest in rules and rituals, sometimes preferring to develop complicated sets of rules of their own. Because they can hold a hand of cards, add up points on dice, and cope with losing, family games become more enjoyable for everyone involved. Fantasy begins to play a smaller role with school-age kids and real-life situations become of greater interest. Craft projects are popular, and kids enjoy making jewelry they can wear or duct tape wallets they can take to school. They enjoy the sense of accomplishment that comes from seeing a project from start to finish.

Simple card games and many board games appeal to kids of this age range. Several different versions of Clue Jr., based on the adult board game Clue, use symbols as well as words so that kids who are just learning to read can solve the puzzles. Oodles of Doodles is a simple, fast-paced introduction to more complicated drawing games, such as Pictionary. Active play is important to kids of this age also. Games like Twister are great and can be played outdoors as well as indoors. They also like throwing at targets and enjoy games involving running, like tag. You also want to find ways to pull kids into non-competitive activities like jigsaw puzzles or family scavenger hunts.

➡ TEN AND UP

Pre-teens develop strong preferences of their own about what kinds of games and activities they want to play. They can be very competitive in these years, and long for challenging strategic and skill-based games. They are able to win and lose with grace, so parents don't have to referee too often. Middle schoolers enjoy games like Are You Smarter Than a 5th Grader? and trivia games intended for their age group. Monopoly is popular with older kids, as is Apples to Apples, The Game of Life, and Pictionary.

 MY STORY

"We try to reinforce skills they are learning at school during our game nights. If they are excited about writing, we let them write the script for a puppet show. If science is something they are involved in at school, we'll try some simple science experiments. We find they're more enthusiastic about family night if we let their areas of interest guide us as far as the activities we choose."

-Sandy, mother of three

• • • • • •

"We let our teenagers select the games we play for our game nights. They usually end up teaching us the rules of some card game they learned from friends, which is an interesting role-reversal. They like being in charge."

-Maria, mother of two

CHAPTER SIX

treats for family fun night

Family Fun Night just wouldn't be the same without a favorite meal or some special snacks. The evening will be especially meaningful to the kids if you invite them into the kitchen: They can assist with the planning, shopping, cooking, and serving. Even though it's a bit more work when kids "help" prepare food, they bring enthusiasm and a refreshing attitude into the kitchen. They are fascinated by how a list of mysterious ingredients like baking soda and shredded lemon peel can combine to create a delicious dish. For them, cooking is less like a chore and more like magic or a really neat science experiment!

five things to have on hand for little chefs

1. A step stool

2. A kid-size apron

3. Hair ties for pulling hair up and out of the way

4. Different colored measuring cups and spoons

5. Small spoons, spatulas, and other kid-size utensils

To make the kids-in-the-kitchen idea work, you'll want to do two things: One is plan ahead, and the other is lower your standards.

Prepare for your little helpers by having specific tasks in mind for them to do and by taking care of much of the work ahead of time. Try to avoid having kids standing around waiting while you tackle a complicated part of the recipe. Before small kids join you in the kitchen, you may want to chop, slice, or puree ingredients, measure them into small bowls, or wash fruits or vegetables.

TIP: Start with something easy to do as a group, like making your own pizza. Kids can choose a crust, add sauce and cheese, and then select their own toppings.

Think about how your kids will be able to contribute and what tasks you can assign to them. Little ones love to stir, knead dough, wash produce, tear lettuce, roll meat into balls, and set the table. Five- to seven-year-olds will be able to take on even more responsibility: They can also read instructions from a recipe card aloud, measure and pour ingredients, and help find things in the kitchen.

Older children will be able to cut vegetables, cheese, or bread; crack eggs; and use a microwave oven or food processor. They will also enjoy putting bite-size pieces of food on skewers. Urge kids who are learning about fractions in school to use their newfound skills to measure ingredients. If they're studying the food pyramid in health class, they can assess the meal and see how it stacks up.

Most teenagers are capable of handling everything themselves, from choosing a recipe to cooking and serving an entire meal. They may want to create their own recipes, try to make an exotic or ethnic dish, or alter existing recipes so that they are vegan or low carb. Encourage their creativity!

Once the meal is underway, relax. Let the kitchen get messy. Don't shoot for a Julia Child creation, just go for edible and interesting. You and the kids will have more fun if you can ignore the sticky floor and the puddle of milk next to the canister set. (Just make sure to include the kids in the clean up, too!)

 # MY STORY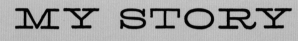

"I learned the hard way that if the kids are measuring ingredients like flour or sugar, I have them do it over a small bowl rather than the mixing bowl so that if they dump too much into the cup, it doesn't spoil the whole thing."

-Helena, mother of two

• • • • • •

"My son always wants to experiment by adding funky ingredients to whatever it is we're making. To avoid ruining an entire meal, I set out a small plastic bowl for him with a portion of the food in it and let him do whatever he wants. Then he can cook or bake his own creation, try it out, and decide if he likes his recipe alterations."

-Eva, mother of one

our family's kitchen rules

You can lighten up about the mess, but be vigilant about safety: Always turn the handles of pots and pans inward so that little kids can't reach up and grab them, and position kids so that they can't reach any appliances or anything sharp. Rather than inundate your children with a list of dos and don'ts, most of which they won't remember, establish a few basic rules, such as:

1. Wash your hands before you begin cooking

2. Don't touch knives without permission

3. Don't use the stove unless supervised

4. _____

5. _____

Many of the Family Fun Night ideas in the upcoming section include suggestions for snacks and special dishes. Kids are just as delighted, however, with take-out food. Most family restaurants offer anything on the menu as a to-go item. If you'd rather focus on the activity than the food, order in (and treat yourself!).

best family fun night recipe: _____

from the kitchen of: _____

SERVES: _____

CHAPTER SEVEN

traditional board game night

Board games have seen a resurgence recently as families rediscover old favorites as well as embrace the newest game crazes. Even though board games have been around for about 7,000 years (the very first games were two-player games like Mancala and chess), board games caught on as a family activity after World War II, with Monopoly, Scrabble, and Parcheesi topping the list of favorites. Not long after, games especially for children, like Candyland and Shoots and Ladders, were introduced.

TIDBIT: Mass-produced board games first appeared in the U.S. in the 1840s and were intended to encourage Christian virtue and principles by rewarding the "right" moves and punishing the "wrong" ones. It wasn't until later that century that Milton Bradley and George S. Parker steered the game industry in a new direction, creating games to be played for fun rather than as a teaching tool.

Trivial Pursuit reignited interest in board games when it burst onto the scene in the 1980s, and sillier games like Pictionary and Imaginiff followed. Recently, technology has infiltrated the board game industry, and many games now include a DVD or computer component.

Even traditional games have been updated and re-imagined to be more relevant and appealing for today's players. Monopoly players can now use credit cards, and play with tokens like leer jets and flat-screen TVs. A new version of Clue has a feature that allows players to text message and a black light that helps with finding clues. New versions of Sorry and Scrabble aimed at today's busy families are designed to last about 20 minutes rather than a few hours.

TIDBIT: Although Charles Darrow gets the credit for bringing the game of Monopoly to the attention of Parker Brothers, many believe that Elizabeth Magie created the original to demonstrate the way landlords abused their tenants. Darrow discovered her game in the early 1930s and changed the locations to familiar places in Atlantic City. The first time he tried to sell it to Parker Brothers, the company rejected it on the basis that it was too complicated. But, like a lot of folks during the Great Depression, Darrow was unemployed and he believed that a game allowing people to amass property and wealth would be a welcome escape from real life. After selling 5,000 games that he made himself, he approached Parker Brothers again. This time the executives were interested. That was a good decision on the part of the company, as 750 million people have played the game since it came on the market in the mid 1930s.

TIDBIT: Monopoly is the best-selling board game in the world:

➡ Over 200 million games have been sold.

➡ Monopoly is sold in 103 countries and in 37 languages.

➡ The longest game on record lasted 70 days.

➡ The longest game in a bathtub (!) lasted 99 hours.

what makes a great board game?

Popular board games may seem to have little in common with one another, but all share several traits that make them stand out.

To begin with, the best games challenge experienced players but are simple enough for new players to enjoy. No one is bored, and no one is frustrated. In addition, rules are not overly complicated, the game moves along at a comfortable pace, and the length of time it takes to play is well suited for the recommended age range.

TIDBIT: In 1931, an out-of-work architect decided to invent a game that was based half on luck and half on skill. After much deliberation, he came up with the idea of Scrabble. He couldn't interest any toy companies in the game, and so for a number of years, he made the games himself for family and friends. He met a man named James Bruno in 1948 who loved the Scrabble idea; Bruno bought the rights and began making games in an abandoned schoolhouse in Connecticut. After losing money for four straight years, he had a bit of luck. Jack Strauss, the chairman of Macy's, the world's largest department store, discovered the game while on vacation in 1952 and ordered some for his store. Today, the game is found in one out of every three American homes and it is sold in 121 countries, making it the world's best-selling word game.

Top games also have flexibility when it comes to the number of players. Enjoyment of the games isn't affected by adding or subtracting players. Also, the best games don't leave anyone out for a significant stretch of time (think musical chairs).

TIDBIT: You might think that Monopoly game you played as a kid is worth big bucks today. Think again. A vintage game's value is determined by how rare it is rather than how old it is. Monopoly games from the 1950s and 1960s are relatively common. You can search eBay's completed auctions to check the prices of games like those you own.

You might not even realize it, but the best games also teach something—trivia facts, money management, or skills like adding or spelling. In addition to inherent educational value, a good game is different each time it's played, making it fun to play over and over again.

Finally, the classic versions of popular games stand up to the test of time. While new versions that pull in pop culture or appeal to tech-savvy teens may be introduced, the original games are still tops.

TIP: Check out these websites to find new games for your family to play:

➡ www.gamewright.com
➡ www.puzzlemethis.com
➡ www.setgame.com

classic family board games

Of the 5,000 games on the market today, only a handful are considered classics: popular, timeless games that your children will likely be playing with their own children someday. Has your family played them all?

CANDYLAND: This is often one of the first games kids learn how to play because only color matching and minimal counting are required. Players race around the board to find the lost King of Candyland.

CHUTES AND LADDERS: Players advance pieces according to a spinner, climbing ladders and heading down chutes. Like many old board games, this one offers a lesson in morality; actions have consequences, both good and bad!

JENGA: Players slide vertically stacked game pieces out one by one; the person who makes the tower fall over loses. Anyone can play—the only skill required is a steady hand!

TROUBLE: The pop-o-matic bubble that holds the die is the most memorable feature of this game! Players race four pieces around a board, hoping to land on an opponent's piece to send it back to the start.

SORRY: Younger players appreciate the simplicity of this game, while older, more experienced players can concoct strategies to trade places and block opponents. No player, however, will be able to get through the game without saying, "Sorry!"

MY STORY

"My kids insist on having alphabet soup on the nights when we play Scrabble. They like the idea of a letter theme!"

-Tina, mother of two

SCRABBLE: A word game for two to four players, Scrabble lets competitors expand their knowledge of vocabulary within an exciting and challenging format. Players score points by using lettered tiles to form words across and down the game board, like a crossword puzzle.

PARCHEESI: Known as a "cross and circle" game with a number of variations played around the world, Parcheesi requires two to four players to move their pawns around the board in a race to the center.

BOGGLE: Using a grid of lettered dice, players must find words in sequences of adjacent letters.

MONOPOLY: Future real estate tycoons ages eight and up will love to amass, trade, and upgrade property. With dozens of pop culture versions, Monopoly can teach kids about bargaining and investing.

CLUE: This clue-based mystery game encourages players to use their problem-solving and reasoning skills to solve a murder. A number of versions are available for different age groups.

YAHTZEE: Success in this simple game hinges on a roll of the dice, but the multiple point combinations reinforce math skills, statistics, and other lessons.

PICTIONARY: Players must draw clues so that their teammates can guess what is written on the chosen card, allowing the team to move ahead on the game board. Artistic skills are not required; often the concept can be conveyed with a clever stick figure or simple sketch. The original game is for ages 12 and up, but there is a junior version available with easier words for younger players. This is a great game for a large group if you set up an easel for drawing.

TIP: Try to come up with your own unique twist to a favorite board game! Pictionary, for instance, can be changed so that every turn is a battle between teams, like an "all play." Or you can challenge the artists by making them draw blindfolded or by poking a pencil through a wrapping paper tube and having a person holding each end as they work together to draw a picture! Be creative!

The twist we add to our favorite game is _____

_____

_____

TRIVIAL PURSUIT: The ultimate trivia game, Trivial Pursuit challenges players to remember facts involving literature, history, sports, and other topics as they try to add plastic subject-area pieces to fill a "pie." Check out the kids' version of this game for ages eight and up or the special editions in a variety of subject areas.

THE GAME OF LIFE: Intended for ages nine and up, Life allows players to manage a mortgage, career choices, insurance, and the unexpected twists and turns of life. A player's choices determine how the game will progress.

CHECKERS: This simple game offers a surprising range of possibilities. Even though it's known as a two-player game, teams can play also, with a leader making the final decision about each move. Your family might also decide to have two or three games going at once, trading players after each round.

TIP: Try giving the familiar game of Checkers a tweak: Tell players that the goal is to get rid of checkers, not accumulate them. How quickly can everyone make the switch?

 MY STORY

"When our daughter was about five, we taught her how to play checkers and then chess because we noticed that she had a hard time thinking a few steps ahead to the consequences of her actions. She was very impulsive. We wanted her to learn—in a fun way—to plan ahead. It worked: She just graduated with honors from Yale."

-Beth, mother of three

some terrific games you may not know about

As delightful as the classics are, don't discount the excellent games available that are not as well known. It can be great fun to "discover" a new game—or to rediscover one you played as a child! Whether your family likes games of strategy, skill, or luck, you'll find a new favorite from among those in our list.

QWITCH: Three to five players race to play cards in sequence in this exciting, "quick switch" game. As letters and numbers go up, down, or remain the same, each player tries to get rid of all of his cards to win. Kids over seven will enjoy this one!

MANCALA: This game of African origin is described as simple to learn and difficult to master, making it suitable for players with a wide range of abilities. Essentially, players must capture as many stones as possible.

TIP: To avoid breaking the bank, trade board games with other families. Write your name on the outside of the box to be sure that anything you lend gets returned!

TIDBIT: Set, Quiddler, and Xactica are produced by the same company, Set Enterprises, Inc. You will feel the brain strain as your mind is challenged in new and interesting ways by these clever, award-winning games.

SET: This challenging "family game of visual perception" has won 25 best game awards, including honors from MENSA, Parents Magazine, and Games Magazine. To begin, twelve or fifteen cards from the Set deck are placed face up, with each card identified by four features (color, number, shape, shading). Players try to identify as many "sets" as possible (a "set" is a group of three cards in which each feature is either the same or different). Younger players are often better at seeing sets than adults!

QUIDDLER: A fast and easy game for kids who know how to read, Quiddler requires players to create words from the lettered cards in their hands. Players try to use the letters with the highest point values. Bonuses are awarded to players who make the most words and the longest word in each round. Games last from 20 to 40 minutes.

XACTICA: The game's slogan is "Beware the Last Card" because of the precision required as players try to predict exactly the outcome of playing eight cards. An innovative version of the popular card game Spades, Xactica is somewhat challenging to learn; there are many rules to game play, but once mastered it's great fun. Families with kids ages 12 and up will enjoy it.

KERPLUNK: Parents might remember this game, which was introduced in the '60s. Straws criss-cross through holes in a plastic tube; marbles are placed on top of the "web" created by the straws. Players take turns removing a straw, trying to prevent marbles from falling out of a hole at the base of the tube. The player who allows the fewest number of marbles to drop wins the game.

APPLES TO APPLES: With a junior version available for kids under 12 as well as the original for adults, this word-association game requires players to make matches with the nouns and adjectives in the deck of cards. The results are often hilarious!

TIP: If you're trying out a game for the first time, have a tried-and-true stand-by in case your family isn't crazy about the new one.

MASTERPIECE: This art auction game is best suited for older kids as the pace might be a bit slow for the littler ones. Strategy and luck combine for moments of excitement and suspense as players discover the value of paintings bought at an "auction": A piece of art might be worth three times what you paid for it, or it might be a worthless fraud! Kids will get a little art history lesson as they learn to recognize classic paintings included with the game.

RAT-A-TAT CAT: A delightful (and delightfully simple) numbers game, Rat-a-Tat Cat boasts charming illustrations on its deck of cards that kids will love. Essentially, each player tries to be the one holding four cards with the lowest total value at the game's end. Warning: The "swap" cards have a way of throwing off everyone's game plan!

SLAMWICH: This award-winning game rewards those with fast hands and sharp eyes, two areas where kids have an advantage over parents! Players will flip, stack, and slap this "loaf" of cards to build slamwiches, each trying to collect as many cards as possible. Slamwich helps teach skills such as visual discrimination and sequencing.

STONE SOUP: In this game based on the popular folk-tale-turned-children's-book, players take turns adding food cards to the "pot" following a certain sequence of ingredients. Like the card game "Liar, Liar" (see page 205), a player may be forced to bluff by adding the wrong card if she doesn't have the one that's needed. You might be surprised at how well your kids can fib!

UGLYDOLL CARD GAME: This easy-to-learn, fast-paced game is similar to Concentration but is essentially a free-for-all, with players grabbing frantically for any matches they see. If your kids are fond of Uglydolls, they'll love it!

TIP: Gamewright, creator of Rat-a-Tat Cat, Slamwich, Stone Soup, and the Uglydoll Card Game was founded in 1994 by four parents who wanted to create top-quality family games with outstanding play value. The company now offers over 50 games and boasts 150 awards. Look for the Gamewright icon—a little joker—on game boxes.

SCENE IT?: This popular DVD board game is full of trivia, on-screen puzzlers, and real clips from movies, TV, music, and sports. There's a Scene It? DVD game for nearly every area of interest.

DICEY: Easy to learn and easy to play, this dice-stacking game requires no skill other than a steady hand. Quick rounds make it a perfect game to include in an evening with several others.

TIDBIT: The spots on dice are called pips!

IMAGINIFF: Do you ever wonder what your family members really think of you? If you were an article of clothing, would they say you were a pair of jeans, a bathrobe, or a ball gown? What if you were a theme park ride? Would you be the bumper cars, a merry-go-round, or a roller coaster? You get the idea! Everyone votes and the most popular answer wins. Up to eight people can play, so it's great for a large family.

CRANIUM: Everyone has a chance to shine in Cranium! Billed as "The Game for Your Whole Brain," Cranium involves teams moving around a board as they complete various activities such as drawing, sculpting, spelling, answering trivia questions, playing charades, or humming. Special editions include Cadoo for kids and Cranium: The Family Fun Game.

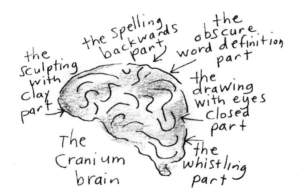

the sculpting with clay part

the spelling backwards part

the obscure word definition part

the drawing with eyes closed part

The Cranium brain

the whistling part

TIP: Families that prefer more involved and complex games should check out strategy games like Parthenon: Rise of the Aegean from Z-Man Games, in which players race to build their civilizations. Vigorous trading, dangerous voyages, and the construction of imposing monuments engage players in this exciting world set in the Aegean Sea in 600 B.C.

TIDBIT: If your family lived in Europe, you might participate in the unlikely yet fascinating sport known as chessboxing. Players alternate between four minutes of chess playing and two minutes of boxing. The game is over when there is a checkmate or a knockout.

Here are our favorite games:

My name is: _____

My favorite game is: _____

because _____

My name is: _____

My favorite game is: _____

because _____

My name is: _____

My favorite game is: _____

because _____

My name is: _____

My favorite game is: _____

because _____

My name is: _____

My favorite game is: _____

because _____

My name is: _____

My favorite game is: _____

because _____

My name is: _____

My favorite game is: _____

because _____

MY STORY

"Our family is small, so we like to invite another family to come over for a pot luck dinner and board games. It works especially well if the other family has a son the same age as ours."

-*Tracie, mother of one*

creating your own special family game

Involve the whole family in creating a game of your very own. You can make an entirely original game or you can alter a favorite game so it has special meaning for your family.

You might start with a board game you already have and talk about how you could change the rules or add or subtract various pieces. Or visit a yard sale and buy several used games; use pieces from each to create a whole new game with a new set of rules. Think big: How about supersizing a game like Checkers? You can paint a checkerboard pattern on a plastic sheet or a large piece of cardboard.

 ## MY STORY

"We play a sort of puzzle game that requires a little preparation. We take song lyrics, proverbs, or pictures from magazines—one item per person—and paste them on pieces of cardboard. Then we cut up each one into at least four pieces. Each person is given one piece of one item, and the others are placed on the table upside down. One at a time, each player turns over a piece to see if it matches the piece he has. If it does, he places it face up on the table; if not, he puts it back. The first one to recreate his song, proverb or magazine picture is the winner."

-Latonya, mother of three

You can also make a unique game from scratch. Think about the kind of games your family likes to play. Do the kids prefer games of luck, strategy, or some combination of the two? Sketch out a rough game board and discuss what the rules should be. It helps to think about what you like and don't like about other games you've played. Study the directions of classic games. You can start with a simple premise of rolling dice and moving game pieces, then add twists and turns to make the game more interesting. Perhaps your game involves your family going on vacation, or getting from home to the zoo. Invent obstacles you might encounter along the way, like a mean dog or nasty neighbor. It's likely that you'll tweak the rules the first few times you play.

TIDBIT: If you think you've created a game other families would enjoy, contact a company that manufactures games and describe your idea. The game Sleeping Queens, sold by Gamewright, was invented by six-year-old Miranda Evarts on a March night in 2003 as she was trying to fall asleep. She imagined a slew of silly queens who needed to be awakened. Miranda and her sister, who are homeschooled, worked with their friends and parents to develop her idea into a working game.

Gamewright receives several hundred ideas every year for new games and accepts about half a dozen of them. According to company executives, the best way to create a top-notch game is to invite friends over to play it with you and offer feedback. Sleeping Queens is Gamewright's first kid-invented game.

If you have an old game board (or can find one at a thrift store or tag sale), you can glue the new game you've designed over the old game. Otherwise, use a piece of white foam board: It's sturdy but lightweight. Be creative with your game board! Use photos of your child's school, favorite restaurant, playground, or even friends and family members. You can also cut out items from magazines that have meaning to you and your kids. For the "start" square, use a photo of your house. Stamps and stickers will make decorating easy. Craft stores sell products that will seal the board once you've finished it to protect it from use. Your kids can come up with clever little items to serve as game tokens, and you can buy dice and cards at a local dollar store. The website www.CustomPlayMoney.com will allow you to personalize play money. If you need cards other than traditional playing cards, use a pack of index cards or blank place cards to make your own.

 # MY STORY

"We play a game called Penny Face. Ahead of time, we make a game card for each player by drawing a face made up of penny-size circles. The winner is the one who fills up his or her face first with pennies. We place a pile of pennies and a deck of cards in the middle of the table. Each person takes turns drawing a card. The cards are valued this way: for an Ace, add two pennies to your face; for a King, Queen, or Jack, add one penny to your face; for sevens, take one penny off of your face and add it to the face of another player; for threes, take one penny away from the face of another player and add it to yours. If you get the five of diamonds, you have to wipe all the pennies off of your face and start again! Other cards have no value. We love our game!"

-Colleen, mother of four

our family's special game

Name: _____

Recommended for ages: _____

Number of players: _____

Playing time: _____

Equipment needed: _____

_____

How to play: _____

_____

_____

_____

_____

_____

_____

This game teaches: _____

_____

_____

Some game manufacturers offer families a way to create their own games based on classics, like Monopoly. Make-your-own-opoly, for instance, allows families to customize a Monopoly game board, cards, play money, and moving pieces with a PC and a color printer. Easy to follow instructions and software will guide you as you create your unique property trading game. If you have a digital camera or scanner, you can add your own photo on the money and game pieces. The game is available at a number of popular online stores for about $25. Check out www.boardgamegeek.com.

A website for Ready-Made Game Boards allows you to download templates to create educational games. Your family can choose clipart or photos to personalize the game. Log onto http://jc-schools.net/tutorials/gameboard.htm to learn more.

If your family wants to explore game-making further, read *Favorite Board Games You Can Make and Play* by Asterie Baker Provenzo and Eugene F. Provenzo (Dover Publications, 1990).

 # MY STORY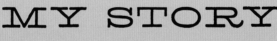

"Our extended family has always loved to play Bingo. It's great because it appeals to the grandparents as well as the littlest ones. We like to make our own cards and have different levels of winning such as filling in the whole card, getting all four corners, or getting a diagonal line."

-Marrin, mother of two

Television game shows are another great inspiration for family games. Play your own version of Wheel of Fortune, for instance. Set up an easel and white board or oversized pad of paper. One person at a time thinks of a phrase, puts blanks representing each letter on the board, and gives a general category like "occupation" or "something found in the kitchen." Each person can guess one letter and, if that letter is in the phrase, take one guess at what the word might be. Think about the game shows your family likes to watch and invent a game based on your favorites!

snack ideas

What's a game night without fun snacks? Here are some tasty ideas:

➡ Make your own Family Fun Night Snack Mix by letting every family member choose an ingredient to add, like peanuts, raisins, pretzels, dry cereal, M&Ms, or marshmallows.

➡ Cut fruit like melons, pineapples, and strawberries into bite-size pieces and let the kids use toothpicks to dip them in:

- whipped cream—alone, or mixed with peach yogurt and finely chopped peaches

- regular or powdered sugar

- melted chocolate

- yogurt, then granola

- 4 ounces of cream cheese whipped, then mixed with a cup of marshmallow fluff

- a cup of crushed macaroon cookies, a cup of sour cream, and 2 tablespoons of brown sugar mixed well together

➡ A plate of raw vegetables can be set out with a variety of dips:

- a favorite salad dressing such as Ranch

- 1 ½ ounce packet of onion soup mix combined with 2 cups of sour cream and 1 ½ tablespoons of Miracle Whip

- 16 ounces of plain yogurt mixed with a packet of Hidden Valley Ranch dressing mix

- flavored whipped cream cheese

- ½ cup of mayonnaise and ½ cup of sour cream mixed with a pinch each of dill weed, parsley, onion flakes, and Beau Monde seasoning

CHAPTER EIGHT

a charitable family fun night

Volunteering together will strengthen your family bonds in a way that is not only fun, but also fulfilling. By volunteering as a family, you can convey to your kids how much they matter— not just to you, but also to the greater community and even to the world. Laying the groundwork for community service pays off: Studies show that people who volunteer when they are young are significantly more likely to volunteer as adults.

For older kids, the concept of a Family Fun Night will be even more appealing if community service is involved. Teens like taking part in real-world activities and feel a genuine sense of satisfaction from helping others. With adult supervision, small children can be valuable helpers, too. According to government surveys, young families and older ones volunteer at about the same rate.

There are all sorts of ways your family can help out on a regular basis in your area, from participating in events with established organizations to creating opportunities to help people you know.

tips for family volunteering

To ensure that your experience is a positive one, take these ideas and strategies into consideration:

1. Match the volunteer opportunity to your family's interests. As a group, brainstorm ideas for helping out.

2. Find a way to help where children are an integral part of the experience, not just relegated to observing or menial jobs. This involves finding out exactly how volunteers are put to use in a given agency.

3. Ask what type of preparation or training is provided for volunteers.

4. Don't over commit at first. You don't have to take on something overwhelming to serve. Find out exactly what will be expected of you. Start small and increase your participation if your family agrees that it would be the right thing for everyone.

5. Be willing to try again if the first situation isn't right for you. Assess what was less than desirable and come up with some other possibilities.

6. Treat it as a job: Show up ready to work and on time. Encourage the kids to step up whenever they notice something needs to be done.

7. Keeping tip #6 in mind, have fun. Let the kids see that you enjoy helping out.

8. Have a family debriefing session when it's all over. Reflect on the experience and ask how everyone felt about it; what they liked and didn't like, and what they feel they gained.

TIP: Consider taking part in National Family Volunteer Day, held each year on the Saturday before Thanksgiving and sponsored by the Points of Light Foundation and Volunteer Center National Network. This day of service was designed to highlight the benefits of family volunteering and to showcase the opportunities available for families wishing to help out in their communities. Families can take part in a variety of community service projects across the country, from park clean-ups to playground building. Visit www. pointsoflight.org for more information.

Your kids may want to visit www.gysd.org to get information on a similar event for young people: Global Youth Service Day, held annually in April.

10 things your kids will get from volunteering with you

1. A greater sense of their role and responsibilities in the community

2. The message that one person can indeed make a difference for the better

3. The satisfaction of realizing that being on the giving end can feel better than being on the taking end

4. A lesson in empathy, respect, and tolerance (many of the families lining up to eat in a soup kitchen don't look that different from our own families)

5. Confidence as they contribute in an adult world

6. Skills they may need in a job someday

7. A sense of empowerment from helping others

8. Greater respect for you, their parents

9. New friends, many of whom will be great role models

10. The opportunity to represent their peers in a positive way

"Every year, our family holds a Box Meal Auction. We invite our friends and neighbors to come and bring a gourmet box lunch (or dinner), wrapped up neatly. Then we auction off each box (with the rule that no one can buy back her own meal). The money we earn goes to fund cancer research."

-Sarah, mother of four

how and where to help

To find a great volunteer opportunity near you, check out local and regional newspapers or community bulletin boards at stores or places of worship. If you don't find anything suitable, visit one of these helpful websites:

www.volunteermatch.org
Post or find volunteer openings that fit your family's needs and abilities.

www.servenet.org
Search the volunteer postings and find local organizations that need your help.

www.idealist.org
This site includes a directory of nonprofit web sites and a database of nationwide opportunities for willing volunteers.

Most states also support websites that list specific volunteer opportunities. The Volunteer Center of Rhode Island's site, for instance, displays over 100 family-friendly postings from agencies statewide. It's important for families to be assertive as they look for ways to serve: One survey reported that even though nearly three-quarters of agencies would be interested in involving family volunteers, 83 percent do not actively recruit them.

ideas for getting involved with an established organization

Some families prefer to sign on with an organization that is already active in the area. Perhaps one of the following suggestions will inspire you.

➡ Sign up for a weekly shift at your local community kitchen. You can cook, serve, or clean up afterward. Usually you will have a time when you can sit and eat with your family and the other volunteers. It's a powerful reminder to your kids about your family's blessings.

➡ If your family loves animals, check with your local animal shelter to see if you can help out. You might be asked to collect old blankets and towels for the animal cages. Often they need volunteers to walk the dogs (and kids usually are required to have parental supervision), making it the perfect family activity.

TIDBIT: Nearly 98 percent of the agencies that used family volunteers found it to be a very effective way to deliver services to those in need, with over 98 percent reporting that families benefitted above and beyond the volunteer experience alone.

➡ Deliver Meals on Wheels to seniors in your community. Visit www.mowaa.org and click on "Take Action" for details.

➡ Do you have a local theater that uses volunteer ushers? Sign up as a group and after you've finished showing patrons to their seats, you can enjoy the performance—for free!

➡ Explore the needs of your local community youth or recreation center, Boys and Girls Club, or YMCA. Perhaps your family can help at the indoor climbing wall, belaying climbers or helping them get into their harnesses. Or you can offer to lead a group on one your favorite family hikes.

➡ From donating blood to helping in times of disaster, the Red Cross has a wide range of needs that families with older kids can help meet. The Red Cross welcomes youth participation, and trains young people to become involved in community disaster education, preparation, and response through the Youth Disaster Corps. Log onto www.redcross.org and click on "Volunteer Your Time" to search for opportunities in your area.

➡ Contact your local DCYF (Department of Children, Youth, and Families) office and ask how you can help the area's foster children. Perhaps you and your kids can donate items in need or decorate duffel bags for kids who move frequently and have no way to carry their things.

➡ You and your older kids can work with Habitat for Humanity, a nonprofit ministry that builds affordable houses for people in need. Visit www.habitat.org to find out how to volunteer in your community.

➤ Is there a cause you believe in as a family? Save the Whales? Greenpeace? Check out groups of interest online and find out if they are organizing peaceful protests or letter-writing campaigns. Every organization can use more sign holders and envelope lickers!

TIDBIT: According to a government survey, about 37 percent of families actively volunteer together. Family volunteering tends to become a tradition once it's been established, with 80 percent of those interviewed continuing to volunteer with relatives.

ideas for creating your own volunteer opportunities

There are a number of things your family can do on its own to serve those in need who live around the corner as well as around the world.

➤ Take an evening to write letters to congressmen and women or other people in positions of power to express your family's opinion about an issue of importance to all of you.

➤ Give a single parent a free night: Invite her kids over to spend the evening with you playing family games!

➤ Pick up trash at a local park or along a walking path (just remember your disposable gloves).

➤ Offer to help an elderly neighbor by raking leaves, weeding a flowerbed, walking his dog, or shoveling the driveway.

➤ Does your family have talent? Entertain seniors at a nursing home or community center with your musical (or other) talents.

➤ Bake cookies and deliver them to the fire department.

TIP: To make cozy blankets you can donate, buy 1 ½ yards of fleece and another 1 ½ yards of fleece in a different, but complementary, pattern and color. Lay one piece on top of the other, with the right sides facing out, and cut a 3-inch long fringe along each side of the doubled-up material. Cut a 3-inch square out of each corner. Assign one family member to each side of the blanket; you will attach the two pieces of fleece together by tying (with a double knot) the top piece of fringe to the one underneath.

➤ Make fleece blankets and donate them to soldiers overseas.

➤ "Adopt" a family living at a homeless shelter and treat the children to a weekly movie, dinner out, or local sporting event.

➤ A family can coach a team: While the parents direct the action on the field, kids can help by keeping score, organizing equipment, and handing out drinks or snacks.

➤ As a family, mentor a child in need. Invite her to dinner, help her with homework and other school projects, and include her in sporting activities.

➤ Adopt a playground: Plant flowers, fix broken equipment, and paint benches.

➤ Computer savvy families can offer to manage the website for a non-profit organization or place of worship.

CHAPTER NINE
movie night

There's more to family movie night than just popping in a DVD from your much-viewed collection! Add a family-run snack bar, unique popcorn treats, and a post-film critics' corner, and you'll create a memorable night for the entire gang.

TIP: Try using popular movie trading sites like www.swapadvd. com: That way, you won't have to invest a lot of money in movies but you can keep them as long as you'd like. The sites work like Netflix, but they are free other than the cost of mailing, which is less than $2. Other sites (such as www.switchplanet.com) also allow users to swap CDs, books, and games.

The trick is to select a movie that appeals to everyone, and not succumb to the temptation to choose a film intended only for kids. That's easier to do if your children are teens and are more likely to agree with you as to what makes a good movie. If your kids are younger (and would argue that there's nothing better than a SpongeBob Square Pants cartoon marathon), then check out the movie list on pages 96-106. These flicks are guaranteed to appeal to all members of the family. To make it more fun, write down the movie titles on slips of paper, fold them, and put them in a jar for a surprise pick. Or take turns choosing movies from our list, or a list that would be acceptable to everyone in your family.

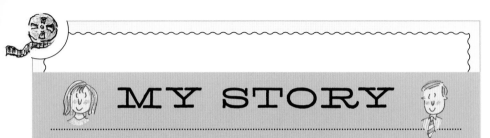

MY STORY

"When our kids were small and insisted on watching animated movies that my wife and I found hard to take, we would play their movie, take an intermission and put them to bed, and then watch our adult feature, like at a drive-in!"

-Glenn, father of three

Get the buzz going early! In the days preceding movie night, promote the film so that your kids are looking forward to it! Hang up a poster (with images downloaded from the Internet) announcing the date, time, and location of your feature presentation. "Pay" the kids in play money throughout the week for good behavior, a kind deed, a chore especially well done, or any positive act. The play money can be used at the snack bar to "buy" popcorn or other munchies or drinks. Buy a roll of tickets like the ones used in movie theaters (from a party or paper goods store) and hand one out to each child a day or two before as his or her ticket to get into the "theater."

On movie night, have the kids put on their pjs, gather sleeping bags and pillows, and set up a cozy spot in front of the sofa. Dim the lights, ask all in attendance to turn off their cell phones, and roll the film!

our favorite family movies are:

_____

_____

_____

_____

_____

_____

_____

_____

_____

 # MY STORY

"For our movie nights, we try to have our meal relate to the film. When we watched _Mulan_, we ate Chinese food (with chopsticks, of course!). For _Ratatouille_, we snacked on baguettes and different kinds of cheese. We find it's a great way to get the kids to try food they normally wouldn't touch!"

-Carrie, mother of four

the snack bar

Set up your kitchen counter like a real theater snack bar! Offer granola bars or fun-size candy bars, as well as small baggies full of candy, trail mix, Chex mix, pretzels, or other treats. Many snacks come pre-packaged in single-serving sizes for lunchboxes. You can also "sell" juice boxes, bottled water, or cans of soda for a special treat. Of course, brown paper lunch bags full of popcorn will likely be the most popular item for your little moviegoers. You can also mix popcorn with peanuts, raisins, and M&Ms to add a little variety.

TIP: To avoid the expense and extra chemicals of microwave popcorn, consider buying a microwave popcorn maker that uses regular popcorn, like the Presto Power Pop (about $20). After the popcorn is made, you can add butter or oil and your own spices like powdered Parmesan and black pepper, curry powder and raisins, soy sauce, coconut flakes, or cinnamon-sugar.

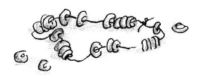

TIP: The night before, the kids can help you make snack necklaces or bracelets to sell at the snack bar. On a piece of new string or licorice, string Honey Nut Cheerios, Froot Loops, and other "O" shaped cereal. Tie the ends to make edible jewelry that the kids can munch on as they watch the movie!

popcorn recipes

Looking for something a little more exotic in the popcorn department? Try these unusual takes on the traditional movie treat.

KETTLE CORN

Ingredients:

1/4 cup vegetable oil

1/4 cup white sugar

1/2 cup unpopped popcorn kernels

Heat the vegetable oil in a large pot over medium heat.

Once the oil is hot, stir in the popcorn and the sugar.

Cover the pot and shake it continuously so that the popcorn and sugar don't burn.

As soon as the popping has slowed down (if you can count to three between pops), take the pot off the stove and shake until the popping has stopped completely.

Dump the popcorn into a large bowl and let it cool. Break up any clusters with a plastic spoon.

For extra fun, add a little food coloring before popping!

CARAMEL CORN

Ingredients:

1 ½ gallons popcorn (popped)

2 cups brown sugar

1 cup butter

½ cup corn syrup

½ teaspoon baking soda

½ teaspoon salt

1 teaspoon vanilla

1 ½ cups peanuts

Preheat oven to 250 degrees.

In a medium-size pan, bring brown sugar, butter and corn syrup to a boil.

Boil gently for 5 minutes without stirring.

Remove the pan from the stove and add the baking soda, salt, vanilla, and peanuts.

Pour over the popcorn and mix until popcorn is coated.

Spread the popcorn on greased cookie sheets and bake for 1 hour, stirring every 15 to 20 minutes.

ZESTY POPCORN

Ingredients:

5 cups popcorn (popped)

5 teaspoons butter, melted

1 teaspoon Italian seasoning

¼ teaspoon garlic salt

3 tablespoons grated Romano or Parmesan cheese

Put the popcorn in a large serving bowl and set aside.

Stir together the butter, Italian seasoning and garlic salt.

Pour the butter mixture over the popcorn and mix well.

Sprinkle with cheese and mix again.

TIP: For a "soda" that mom will like better, try mixing fruit juice (like grape or cranberry) with club soda or ginger ale.

TIP: You can look up fun facts to share with your family about the movies that you watch together by going to the Internet Movie Database (www.imdb.com) and clicking on "trivia" (under the heading "Fun Stuff" in the left-hand column of the page). Here are some facts that you might find there:

➡ Anna Popplewell, the actress who plays the oldest sister, Susan Pevensie, in *The Chronicles of Narnia*, is terrified of mice! As a result, every scene in which Susan interacts with mice had to be shot with her stunt double.

➡ The original script of *Remember the Titans* was full of profanity, but Disney refused to release the movie until every swear word was removed from the script.

➡ John Travolta plays a woman in *Hairspray* (he plays the main character's mother), and it took him four hours each day to put on the fat suit and make-up.

➡ In *Night at the Museum*, there are scenes in which Ben Stiller's character, Larry, interacts with a miniature figure of a cowboy named Jedediah, played by Owen Wilson. During filming, Stiller filmed every scene with Jedediah by talking to a toothpick, and special effects teams added in Wilson later.

➡ In *Fly Away Home*, the aircrafts used in the movie were the actual aircrafts used by the real-life team to help the geese migrate south!

MY STORY

"We lay out an old blanket and set up a picnic dinner in the middle of the family room while we watch our movie. My kids swear that the food tastes better when they eat it that way!"

-Rhea, mother of three

the best
family movies

It can be hard for parents to determine just by reading a synopsis whether a movie will hold everyone's interest. That's why the movies on this list (all rated G or PG) are regarded as universal: parents, teens, and younger kids will all find them appealing. As kids get older and graduate to PG13- and R-rated movies, they will want to recommend films for movie night, but until then, here are some great choices.

Chronicles of Narnia: The Lion, The Witch, and The Wardrobe

- Rated PG for battle sequences and frightening moments
- 143 minutes
- Oscar winner
- Based on the classic novel
- A visually stunning adventure tale with epic battle scenes that boys, especially, will love

The Incredibles

- Rated PG for action violence
- 115 minutes
- Winner of two Oscars, including Best Animated Feature of the Year
- A family of undercover superheroes tries to blend in with society as they come together to save the world

Wall-E

- Rated G
- 98 minutes
- Oscar winner for Best Animated Feature Film
- A timely message about environmental responsibility and sustainability, along with an irresistible love story, make this animated movie one that speaks to parents as well as kids

October Sky

- Rated PG for language, brief teen sensuality and alcohol use, and for some thematic elements
- 108 minutes
- A heartwarming and inspirational true story about a young boy who must fight against the expectations of his family (especially his father) and his community in order to follow his dream of flying rockets

Finding Nemo

- Rated G
- 104 minutes
- Oscar winner for Best Animated Feature Film; second-highest grossing animated film of all time (behind Shrek 2)
- A touching journey of a father searching for his son with the always-funny Ellen DeGeneres as the voice of Dory

Hairspray

- Rated PG for language, some suggestive content, and momentary teen smoking

- 117 minutes

- Based on the Broadway musical

- A fun, feel-good musical that promotes the value of a positive self-image, with special appeal for pre-teen and teen girls

Swiss Family Robinson

- Not rated, but we'd give it a PG rating for mild peril

- 126 minutes

- A family classic, originally released in 1960

- A family shipwrecked on a deserted island must work together to survive: What would YOUR family do in their shoes?

Ice Age

- Rated PG for mild peril

- 81 minutes

- Parents will love the comedy of Ray Romano as the voice of the main character, a wooly mammoth who refuses to migrate south in preparation of the impending ice age (while kids will prefer the tribe of zany Dodo birds)

Shrek (and Shrek 2)

- Rated PG for mild language and some crude humor

- 90 minutes

- Oscar winner for Best Animated Feature Film

- Based on William Steig's fairy tale picture book, with Eddie Murphy as the hilarious donkey, this film combines adult-oriented humor, a kid-friendly plot, and a great soundtrack

The Love Bug

- Rated G

- 107 minutes

- Herbie, a Volkswagen beetle with a mind of its own, is the charming hero of the film from 1968 as well as the latest sequel, released in 2005, starring Lindsey Lohan

Kung Fu Panda

- Rated PG for sequences of martial arts action

- 92 minutes

- This movie, about a lazy panda who is chosen to become a kung-fu master to protect his way of life, features the voices of Jack Black, Dustin Hoffman, and Angelina Jolie

The Princess Bride

- Rated PG for mild peril, some action violence
- 98 minutes
- This charming, quirky cult-classic-turned-mainstream-film will appeal to boys as much as girls because of elaborate sword fights, giants, and an evil prince

The Absent-Minded Professor (or Flubber)

- Rated G
- 97 minutes
- A bumbling chemistry professor/inventor creates "flubber," anti-gravity goop that leads to some hilarious misadventures
- The latest version stars Robin Williams and is called *Flubber*

Monsters, Inc.

- Rated G
- 92 minutes
- Oscar winner for Best Original Song
- Monsters who have to make kids scream and harness the energy in order to fuel their city are actually terrified of children in a clever plot twist designed to help younger kids overcome their fear of monsters
- Parents and older kids will enjoy the comedy of Billy Crystal and John Goodman, who voice the principal characters

My Dog Skip

- Rated PG for some violent content and mild language
- 95 minutes
- A shy boy comes into his own with the help of a new terrier puppy, set in 1940s Mississippi
- A charming and entertaining movie for dog-lovers of any age, especially boys

Because of Winn-Dixie

- Rated PG for thematic elements and brief mild language
- 106 minutes
- Based on the award-winning book, this film tells the story of a lonely girl who finds a dog in the supermarket and, thanks to the friendly mutt, makes an assortment of new friends and gains insight into different kinds of people
- A great dog movie for girls, who may want to read the book first

Ghostbusters

- Rated PG for thematic elements, mild language, and some scary images
- 105 minutes
- Consistently ranks in top 100 greatest comedy films lists
- Three eccentric, unemployed parapsychologists (two played by Dan Ackroyd and Bill Murray) set up shop to exterminate the city's pesky ghosts and goblin

Night at the Museum

- Rated PG for mild action, language, and brief rude humor
- 108 minutes
- Ben Stiller is outrageously funny as the new night security guard at the Museum of Natural History who discovers that an ancient curse causes the exhibits to come to life and run wild through the building

Mulan

- Rated G
- 88 minutes
- A Disney classic that doesn't reinforce the helpless damsel-in-distress stereotype, *Mulan* features a Chinese maiden who goes to battle dressed as a man in order to save her father's life. Her heroism will inspire young girls and boys will love the epic battle sequences (though they'll merely tolerate the singing)

Back to the Future

- Rated PG for thematic elements and some language
- 117 minutes
- Oscar winner
- Time travel permits Marty McFly to reappear in 1955, but when he accidentally prevents his parents from getting together, he realizes that if he doesn't correct his mistake, he'll never exist!
- A family classic with two sequels

Remember the Titans

- Rated PG for thematic elements and some language
- 113 minutes
- This inspirational true story follows a newly appointed African-American coach as he helps his high school team through their first season as a racially integrated group

Groundhog Day

- Rated PG for some thematic elements (this film may receive a PG-13 rating today, so it may not be appropriate for the younger kids)
- 101 minutes
- A weatherman (the always-funny Bill Murray) finds himself living the same day over and over again until he realizes that he must reexamine his priorities and make some changes in his self-indulgent lifestyle

Toy Story

- Rated G
- 81 minutes
- A charming cast of characters (with Tom Hanks as the voice of the hero) tell the story of a cowboy doll that is extremely jealous when a spaceman action figure takes his place as the favorite toy in a boy's room
- If you like this movie, put *Toy Story 2* on your list

The Iron Giant

- Rated PG for fantasy action and mild language

- 86 minutes

- This animated film, both heart-warming and hilarious, follows the adventures of a boy who befriends a gentle giant robot that a paranoid government agency has decided it must eliminate

It's a Wonderful Life

- Unrated (though it would likely earn a PG rating today)

- 130 minutes

- This black and white family classic, released in 1946, tells the story of an angel who helps a kind but despairing man by showing him how different life in his hometown would have been if he had never existed

The Wizard of Oz

- Unrated (though it would likely earn a PG rating today for some scary images)

- 101 minutes

- Winner of two Oscars

- In this well-loved musical, Dorothy and her dog Toto are swept away by a tornado and dropped into a fantasy land where they must embark on a journey to find the wizard in order to return home

E.T.

- Rated PG for language and mild thematic elements
- 115 minutes
- Winner of four Oscars
- A tearjerker and timeless classic, *E.T.* follows a group of children who try to help a stranded alien return home before government agents capture him

The Greatest Game Ever Played

- Rated PG for some brief mild language
- 120 minutes
- The true story of the 1913 U.S. Open in which Francis Ouimet, an amateur golfer from a blue collar background, refuses to give up on his dream of playing in one of the country's most prestigious golf tournaments

National Treasure

- Rated PG for action violence and some scary images
- 131 minutes
- Nicolas Cage stars as a roughneck hero on a quest for an ancient treasure whose first task is to steal the Declaration of Independence

Fly Away Home

- Rated PG for an initial accident scene (warning: might upset young viewers) and some mild language

- 107 minutes

- This touching movie is based on the true story of a teenage girl who loses her mother in an accident and must move in with her father. Life is miserable for Amy until she finds abandoned goose eggs and raises the baby geese. When winter comes, Amy and her father (and his special invention) will join forces to help the birds fly south

TIP: Curious to know if the movie you chose had any major blunders? A caveman wearing a wristwatch? A tattoo that mysteriously disappears mid-movie? Go to the Internet Movie Database (www.imdb.com) and type a movie name in the search bar. Scroll halfway down the page where you'll see a running bar on the left-hand side of the page labeled "Fun Stuff." Check out the "Goofs" section under that category.

after the movie

You can use movie review sites to jumpstart a great conversation after the movie ends (as well as to help you decide which movies your family will watch in the future). Print out the reviews ahead of time and have them handy as the final credits roll. Don't feel that your kids are too young to be movie critics: Even a five-year old can discuss and analyze a film.

These three sites offer different levels of reviews and different types of information. Choose the one that best suits your family's needs and interests:

➡ www.allmovie.com:
This is the most sophisticated of the three sites, with in-depth film reviews by respected critics that delve into trends within the genre, cinematography, sub-texts, themes, and tone as well as offering easy-to-understand ratings of one to five stars. A family of true film buffs will appreciate the information offered by this high-quality database.

➡ http://rogerebert.suntimes.com:
Well-respected film critic Roger Ebert writes reader-friendly reviews based on performances and plot lines. Check out his One-Minute Movie Reviews for a cut-to-the-chase film analysis.

➡ http://movies.yahoo.com:
This site is the most universal of the three, with basic and easily accessed information about each movie. Search "movies" and click on the desired movie title, then check out a plot synopsis, user reviews, or reviews by well-known critics. Every movie receives an average letter grade by both critics and reviewers and lists how much money it made at the box office.

TIP: You don't have to be a film studies professor to lead an interesting discussion about a movie you've just seen. Here are five basic questions to get everyone talking:

1. If the main character were a real person, would he or she be your friend? Why or why not?

2. Would you have made the same choices that the main character did? Why or why not?

3. What moment in the movie will you remember the most?

4. What about the movie surprised you?

5. Is there another ending you could imagine?

Don't overlook the special commentary or bonus features section of the movie! (A later release of a film is more likely to have special features.) You'll find a lot of substance there, with "making of" scenes, director's commentary, interviews with the actors, and deleted scenes. A director may comment on why a scene was deleted. Does your family agree with his or her decision? You may learn why an actor decided to take on a certain role, or why an action scene was filmed the way it was.

For example, on the two-disc special edition of *Chronicles of Narnia*, a special feature shows viewers how each of the creatures was created through make-up, costumes, and special effects like green screen. Interested in knowing how the Minotaurs or goblins evolved from sketches to final realization? Find "Evolution of an Epic" and click on "Creating Creatures." You'll be amazed!

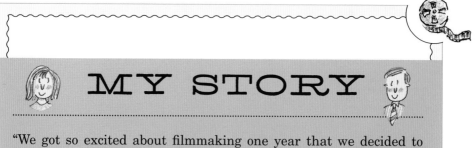

MY STORY

"We got so excited about filmmaking one year that we decided to make our own movie. We wrote up a script and my husband filmed while the rest of us acted it out. My oldest daughter used a program on her computer to edit it and add music. It turned out great!"

-Maryanne, mother of five

CHAPTER TEN

family fun night picnic

It's hard to go wrong with a picnic basket full of food and drinks, a bucolic setting, and a host of delightful games for your family to play!

the perfect picnic spot

You'll want to pick a setting for your picnic that will allow your kids to take part in the activities that they enjoy. You might decide to head for a schoolyard after hours where you'll have access to playground equipment, a baseball diamond, or a soccer field. You might choose a public beach where you can play water games and swim. Or you may prefer a nearby public park with pavilions, picnic tables, and built-in barbeque grills.

TIP: Don't forget to bring

➡ Garbage bags

➡ Can opener, bottle opener

➡ Serving spoons

➡ Serrated knife, cutting board

➡ Folding chairs

➡ Sunglasses, visors, hats

➡ Sweatshirts, jackets

➡ Wipes to clean up after the meal

➡ Roll of paper towels

➡ Plastic wrap, baggies, and plastic containers for leftovers

➡ Picnic blanket

➡ Beach towels

➡ Insect repellant

➡ Sunscreen (if heading out mid-afternoon)

➡ Basic first aid kit

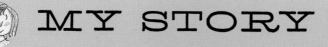
"Our family tries to picnic 'green,' that is, in an environmentally-friendly way. Sometimes we bike to our picnic spot rather than drive; other times we use cloth napkins and plates and silverware that we take back home. We always pack food in re-usable containers rather than plastic bags and we fill our own water bottles before we leave so we don't throw away plastic bottles. Our goal is to combine enjoying the outdoors with respecting the environment."

-Serena, mother of four

your picnic dinner

Whether you bring along a gourmet spread or sandwiches from Subway, food eaten outdoors just tastes better! Keep it simple (think bite-size whenever possible), and bring just what you'll eat and no more. A deli bar is easy and popular: Pack assorted meats, cheese, rolls, condiments and pasta salads in vinegar-based marinades. Round out the meal with pretzels or chips, carrot and celery sticks, grapes, slices of watermelon, and cookies or Rice Krispie treats. Cold chicken is another picnic favorite, served with a side of potato salad and fresh fruit kabobs. Trail mix is a great pre- or post-meal snack.

TIDBIT: If you want to keep the bugs away from you and your kids, don't feed everyone bananas! Mosquitoes love the scent of your skin after you've eaten a banana. Conversely, adding a bit of garlic to the meal will cause you to emit an odor that helps keep the bugs away. And if you avoid using scented soap or shampoo, the mosquitoes will search the park for sweeter smelling targets.

TIP: The best tips for picnic dinners

In advance

 Freeze water bottles to pack between (not just under) food items; they will keep food cold but will melt by the end of the evening for cold drinking water

➡ Save individual packets of mayo, mustard, and ketchup from fast food restaurants to bring on the picnic

➡ Make sure the chosen location does not have restrictions that will affect your plan (regarding barbeque grills, pets, swimming...)

➡ Check the weather forecast

On the day of

➡ Envision yourself at the picnic site eating the meal to make sure you don't forget to pack something critical, like a serving spoon or bottle opener

➡ Pack foods to be eaten last on the bottom of the cooler

➡ Bring two coolers, one for drinks and one for food (because the one holding drinks will be opened more often)

➡ Use pita bread "pockets" to hold sandwich fillings

You can certainly have a traditional cookout with burgers and hot dogs, but you'll have to pay special attention to keeping meat cold until it's time to put it on the grill. You'll also have to be prepared for a wait as the charcoal heats up.

TIP: Tips for cooking on a charcoal grill

➡ Marinate the meat the night before and wrap it in plastic wrap.

➡ Use a wire brush to clean the grill.

➡ With a paper towel, rub a little vegetable oil on the grill so the meat doesn't stick.

➡ Use an electric charcoal lighter rather than lighter fluid to avoid adversely affecting the food's flavor.

➡ When the coals are red, spread them out using tongs. For direct cooking, coals are spread evenly over the bottom of the grill; for indirect cooking, the charcoal is placed on the sides of the grill bottom, but not in the center. After about 20 minutes, they will turn white-ish; then they're ready. Cedar chips for flavoring can be placed directly on coals or in a perforated foil pouch under the grill surface.

➡ Cook hot dogs, hamburgers, corn on the cob, and potatoes over direct heat. Thicker meats like steak and chicken quarters can be cooked over indirect heat. Allow four minutes on each side for a burger, and about an hour and a half for chicken (until the juices run clear).

➡ Turn the meat after one side has finished cooking; when cooked through, remove the meat with a clean set of tongs.

here are some recipe ideas to try for your next picnic

CORN ON THE GRILL

Ingredients:

Fresh ears of corn, husks on

Butter

Salt

With the husks on, soak ears of corn in water for 15 minutes.

Place the corn directly on the grill, rotating the ears with tongs as they cook for 10 to 15 minutes, depending on how hot the coals are.

Remove from the heat and peel carefully.

Butter and salt to enhance the flavor.

BURGERS
WITH A TWIST

Ingredients:

1 egg, beaten

½ cup breadcrumbs

¾ cup shredded cheddar cheese

3 green onions, chopped

2 tablespoons Worcestershire sauce

1 tablespoon mustard

Dash pepper

1 ¼ pounds ground beef

Combine the egg, breadcrumbs, cheese, green onions, Worcestershire sauce, mustard, and pepper.

Add the ground beef and mix. Shape into four patties.

Grill over direct heat.

Serve on toasted buns.

WATERMELON BOWL
FRUIT SALAD

Ingredients:

Watermelon, cut in half

Fresh fruit, cut into bite size chunks

Hollow out the half-watermelon.

Scoop the fruit salad into the watermelon bowl. If you like, you can slide some pieces of fruit onto skewers and arrange the kabobs to come out of the watermelon bowl.

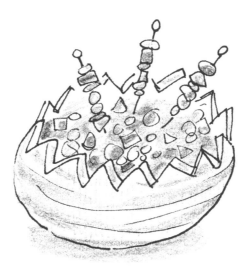

WALDORF SALAD

Ingredients:

2 to 3 cups chopped apple

1 cup cheddar cheese chunks

1 cup seedless grapes

½ cup diced celery

½ cup chopped walnuts

½ cup raisins

⅓ cup mayonnaise

2 teaspoons sugar

dash allspice

1 tablespoon lemon juice

In a large bowl, mix the apple, cheese, grapes, celery, walnuts and raisins.

Combine the mayonnaise, sugar, allspice, and lemon juice; add to the apple mixture, stirring well.

Keep cold until ready to serve.

TIP: Items to bring along for fun

→ Flying disc, like a flexible, glow-in-the-dark Frisbee

→ Large ball or beach ball

→ Foxtail Softie

→ Bottles of bubbles

→ Butterfly or fishing net

→ Binoculars

→ Containers for holding bugs and other critters for observation

→ Flashlights for tag

→ Water pistols

→ Badminton set

→ Jump ropes

→ Water balloons

→ Kites

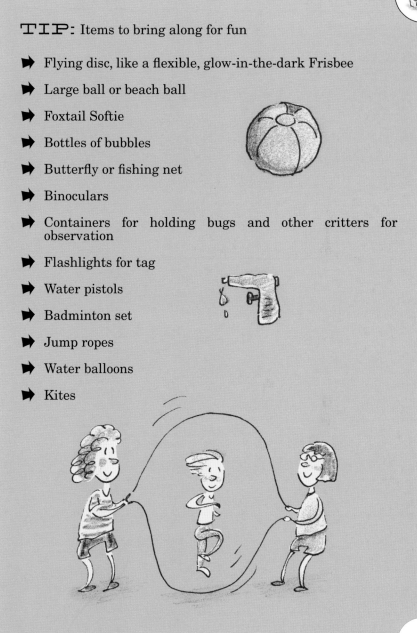

TIP: Play these fun games with your kites!

➡ Have a contest to see whose kite can fly the highest in one minute.

➡ Follow the leader: One kite leads the way, and the others try to follow its path.

➡ Have a relay race! Divide your family into two teams, each with a kite. One at a time, members of each team must make the kite do a figure eight in the air, then pass the handle to the next person. The team to finish first wins!

➡ Compete with the other kite flyers to see whose will be the last kite flying. No interfering with the other contestants!

games to play at your family picnic

Hide-and-seek is fun to play the old-fashioned way, but there are variations that can make it even more interesting...

SARDINES: One person is chosen to hide as the others cover their eyes and count to 25. As each person finds the initial hider, she joins him, so that more and more people are crowding into one hiding spot. The one who spotted the hider first is the one who hides in the next round.

KICK THE CAN: One person is named "It." It places an empty can, water bottle, or whatever is handy in a central location and counts to 25 (eyes covered) while the others hide. When It finds someone hiding, that person must return to the location marked by the can. Any player who hasn't been found can sneak over and kick the can, allowing everyone to hide again (including anyone who has been caught). All players are safe until It sets the can back up. The game ends when everyone has been found; the first person to have been caught becomes It in the next round.

TIP: Forget to bring what you need to play games? Get creative! Fill someone's sock with playground or beach sand, tie a knot at the top, and use it instead of a ball or Foxtail Softie.

Tag is more fun when it's played with some different rules...

CHAIN TAG: The player who is It starts running after the others and when she tags someone, that person must hold hands with her. Together, they try to catch someone else. When they do, that person must join hands with them. This leaves just the two "outer" free hands in the line for tagging. When everyone has been tagged, the first player to have been caught becomes the next It.

SHADOW TAG: Rather than tagging another player out, It must step on the person's shadow; then she becomes It.

BALL TAG: It throws a playground ball at the others; they are out when the ball hits them.

WATER PISTOL TAG: It shoots at the other players with a water pistol; anyone who gets hit by the stream of water is out.

MY STORY

"We play a special kind of tag that helps to alleviate fighting among the kids. We call it Hug Tag and the idea is that players cannot be tagged by It if they are hugging another player!"

-Steve, father of three

MONKEY-IN-THE-MIDDLE TAG: It stands in the middle of a circle as a ball is tossed from one player to another. It tries to tag the player who is holding the ball.

A traditional race can be a bit ho-hum. Try one of these variations…

WAIST RACE: This race works well for groups of six or more…and it's hilarious! Players on each team line up one behind the other, with each one holding onto the waist band of the person in front of him. On "go," each team runs to a designated line at least 50 yards away, with all players hanging on to one another. If someone lets go or falls, the other team wins!

ONE-MINUTE RACE: Designate a racecourse that is relatively short and assign one person to be the timer. As the racers line up, they must relinquish their watches. On "go," everyone walks or runs the course, with the goal of completing the loop in exactly one minute. The slowest person might win—or the fastest! It depends on who is best able to figure out how long a minute is!

TIP: Other ways to have outdoor fun

➡ Use water pistols to squirt at balloons and keep them up in the air

➡ Use water pistols to squirt a beach ball into the opponent's end zone: a bit like soccer, without the kicking!

➡ Play touch football with a water balloon rather than a football

➡ Swing a jump rope in a low circle (like a helicopter propeller); each player jumps over it when it swings near him

➡ Play monkey-in-the-middle with a beach ball, Frisbee, or Foxtail softie

 # MY STORY

"We play a game that is like badminton but is called Doink It. Players have more control because the Doink It ball is easier to aim than a birdie. It also travels farther and is less affected by the wind. The paddles are very similar to those used for badminton. We bought our set at a store specializing in games and puzzles."

-Rawan, mother of three

TIP: How to skip stones

It's all about selection, spin, and speed. Choose stones that are smooth, uniformly thin and flat, and that fit easily into your hand. (Triangular stones work best for choppy waters.) Stand with the shoulder of your non-throwing arm facing the water, feet shoulder-width apart. Stretch your throwing arm backwards and then swing it toward the water, extending your arm and releasing the stone with a quick wrist snap. The stone should spin across the water, with the first skip about five yards away.

SPUR-OF-THE-MOMENT RELAY RACE:

Find two crooked sticks, each about a foot in length. Divide the group into two teams and establish a start line and a finish line. Players on each team take turns kicking the stick to the finish line and back until everyone on the team has had a turn. The first team to finish wins. (This is an old Native American game.)

Volleyball has a number of variations. Decide which one would work best with your group...

BEACH BALL VOLLEYBALL:

Use a beach ball rather than a standard volleyball. If it's windy, it'll add a chaotic element that can be fun. If it's a calm day and you have littler kids, they'll be more likely to be able to hit a lightweight beach ball.

TIP: To make a volleyball game more cooperative and less competitive, divide the group into two random teams. As soon as a person hits the ball over the net, he scoots under the net to join the other team. Eventually, the teams will be entirely different from the starting teams and no one will have won or lost.

ALL-TOUCH VOLLEYBALL:

No one will feel left out in this version: The ball can't be sent back over the net until every person on a side has touched it.

TOWEL-LY BALL:

This works well with four people of mixed ages, with two on each side. Partners hold a towel stretched out between them, tossing and catching the ball using only the towel. You can make it more challenging by having two balls going at once.

WATER VOLLEYBALL:

In this derivation, players sit in inner tubes to hit the ball back and forth so that kids who aren't strong swimmers can play (with supervision), too.

CHAPTER ELEVEN

video game night

When public libraries across the country recently sanctioned video games, many parents grudgingly relented, too. On National Gaming Day, libraries included a nation-wide video game tournament as well as the traditional board game competitions, an acknowledgement that video games have become an integral part of our society.

 MY STORY

"My son's favorite part of family video game night is that he teaches everyone else how to play the games. His sisters are learning, but he's definitely the expert. As the youngest child, he rarely has the opportunity to show the rest of us how to do something."

-Kendra, mother of three

Even though many parents are reluctant to join the video game revolution, others are happy to get in on the act, viewing it as an opportunity to bond with pre-teens and teens and to model for them balance and restraint. These parents feel that they can show their kids how quality video games can be enjoyed in moderation. In addition, playing games together allows technology to unite the family rather than isolate kids so that they withdraw.

You may go along with the video game idea half-heartedly, but chances are you'll find at least one or two games that appeal to you. No longer the domain of pre-adolescent boys, video games have become popular family entertainment. Believe it or not, studies have shown that women make up 40 percent of the gaming community! Parents soon find themselves getting excited about the idea of hitting a home run, drag racing, or singing in a rock band—without leaving the family room!

More than 40 percent of households now own at least one video game system. Especially popular with families is the Nintendo Wii, which attracts non-gamers with its user-friendly wand (rather than a multi-button controller). The Wii is touted as the "new family bonding experience"; over 13 million of these systems have been sold in the United States. Almost 90 percent of the time, Wii players are playing with another person in the family. And the other person isn't necessarily a sibling: One-third of those who own a Wii admit to frequently playing games with their parents and nine percent play with grandparents! (Many senior citizen centers are now equipped with Wii systems for bowling, golf, and baseball tournaments!)

TIDBIT: Almost twice as many women as teen boys play video games! The Entertainment Software Association reports that 18 percent of boys play video games compared to 33 percent of women! Studies have even shown that women were more "dedicated" players, meaning that they averaged more online hours per week (29) than men (25).

TIDBIT: Classic board games have gone digital, too! In the spring of 2009, games like Boggle, Connect Four, and Battleship became available in Xbox Live Arcade formats. A video game version of Cranium (Cranium Kabookii) is available on the Wii platform. The activities include some elements of the original game as well as some new aspects that are more appropriate for a video game format.

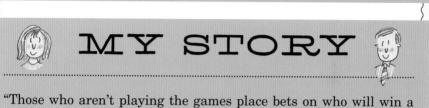

MY STORY

"Those who aren't playing the games place bets on who will win a drag race or bowling match... That makes it more fun to watch!"

-Stacie, mother of four

choosing a game system

The top three video-game systems—the Wii, Xbox 360, and Playstation 3 (PS3)—are actually quite different from one another. Before you settle on a system, you'll want to think about your family's needs.

The Wii, with its wealth of kid-friendly titles, is best suited for those interested in more active games with their families. Intense gamers opt for the Xbox 360, and the PlayStation is best for families who are also interested in multimedia and movie-watching features. The PlayStation has a built-in Blu-ray player and allows viewers to download movies through Sony's PlayStation Network video service. (The Xbox Live allows users to stream high-def movies from Netflix.) In addition, some consoles are known for specific games, so your family will want to consider what games are of greatest interest.

If price is a consideration (and when isn't it?), then you may be influenced by the relatively low cost of the Wii, at about $250. The Xbox (not the Xbox Arcade) from Microsoft ranges in price from $300 to $400. Sony's PlayStation 3 tops the price list at between $400 and $500.

ideas for great family games

One big reason that video games have become more popular with families is the greater diversity of games. Games are no longer limited to hurling grenades or jabbing with swords; manufacturers of the top three systems offer an incredible variety of game themes—from yoga to ghost-busting to drag racing. Perhaps the most popular family titles currently are Rock Band and Guitar Hero (available on all three consoles). Nearly everyone harbors a fantasy of singing or strumming on stage before a legion of faithful fans!

Pay close attention to the ratings provided by the Entertainment Software Rating Board when selecting a game for the family to play. They are extremely helpful when trying to determine the specific contents of a game: Some are family-friendly while others have themes much too mature for a young audience.

TIP: If you and your kids know what the Entertainment Software Rating Board (ESRB) ratings mean, you'll be able to choose games that you feel are appropriate for your family. The ratings are intended to provide information about the content of games and have two parts: the rating symbol (on the front) that suggests an age range and the content descriptor (on the back) that indicates aspects in a game that may be of concern. The most frequently used ratings are:

EC (Early Childhood)
Games are suitable for children three and up. There is nothing that would cause parents concern.

E (Everyone)
Games are aimed at children six and older. There may be minimal animated or fantasy violence or mildly inappropriate language.

E10+ (Everyone 10 and older)
Titles may include more cartoon, fantasy, or mild violence and mildly offensive language. There may also be limited suggestive themes.

T (Teen)
Games are appropriate for those 13 and over. These titles may contain violence, suggestive themes, offensive humor, limited blood, simulated gambling, and limited strong language.

M (Mature)
Titles are aimed at those 17 and up. Games rated "M" may include violence, blood and gore, sexual content, and strong language.

Content descriptors include a wide range of elements from alcohol and drug references to nudity.

MY STORY

"We always rent a game before we buy it, just to make sure it will be appropriate for the kids and challenging enough for Bill and me. New games often cost $50 or more, so a mistake can be costly."

-Margaret, mother of two

The following list represents just a sampling of the many family-friendly titles. Though the games are categorized according to game systems, a number of titles are available in multiple platforms.

TIP: Wii Sports, one of the most popular family games, is currently included with the Wii game system and boasts five major games: bowling, boxing, baseball, golf, and tennis.

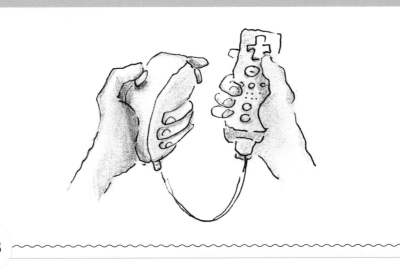

games for the wii

Endless Ocean: Dive, Discover, Dream

Diving partners search for buried treasure and encounter fascinating sea creatures as they explore the deep sea in this underwater adventure.

ESRB rating: E

Animal Crossing: City Folks

Up to four players create their own unique story line in a virtual village, chatting with neighbors, gardening, collecting items for their homes, or hopping onto a bus for an adventure. There's no high score, or even end to the game, just relaxed, leisurely fun.

ESRB rating: E for Comic Mischief

TIP: If you're thinking of buying another Wii controller, consider buying Wii Play, which consists of nine arcade-type games and includes a wand. You'll pay $50 and, considering that the wand is worth $40, that makes the game a steal at $10.

De Blob

Superhero de Blob must battle Inkies and launch a full-scale revolution to colorize the dull, lifeless Chroma City. Older as well as younger kids will enjoy the audio and visual effects as they compete for control of Chroma City in four-player split screen.

ESRB rating: E for Mild Cartoon Violence

Sonic Riders: Zero Gravity

Sonic the Super Hedgehog returns in this new racing game with tricky courses and anti-gravity moves.

ESRB rating: E for Cartoon Violence

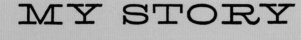 MY STORY

"My kids love the game Playground because it has familiar activities like tetherball, dodge ball, and darts—things that kids get excited about in real life. Adults are challenged but kids are able to keep up."

-Greg, father of two

Mario Kart Wii

Mario, Yoshi, Donkey Kong, and others are back to race around the track! Younger children who have not quite mastered the Wii wand will appreciate the simplicity of this game, which involves pressing a "go" button and steering.

ESRB rating: E for Comic Mischief, Mild Animated Violence

Wii Fit

"Exergame" through yoga, aerobics, balance games, push ups, and other forms of exercise. This game provides enjoyment as well as fitness, making it perfect for families cooped up inside who are yearning for a reason to jump around!

ESRB rating: E for Comic Mischief

Wario Ware: Smooth Moves

Active participation and quirky, unique scenarios make this a great family or party game. Jump (literally!) over hurdles, run a relay race, or copy dance moves, teaming up with or competing against other players. Move the furniture before you start!

ESRB rating: E 10+ for Crude Humor, Mild Cartoon Violence

Smarty Pants: Trivia Fun for Everyone!

Because trivia questions are automatically tailored to each individual player, this game is perfect for families with diverse abilities. Players can play collaboratively or competitively, answering over 20,000 questions. But don't get the idea that it's too sedentary: Players spin category wheels, have tug-of-wars, and compete in dance-offs!

ESRB rating: E for Alcohol and Tobacco Reference

Lego Star Wars: The Complete Saga

This popular family game (requiring creative thinking and cooperative play to solve puzzles) allows players to experience events of all six Star Wars movies in one game.

ESRB rating: E 10+ for Cartoon Violence

Super Smash Bros. Brawl

As Pikachu, Sonic the Hedgehog, or Mario, gamers can battle family members sitting next to them or friends across the country via the online multiplayer option! There may not be too much educational value in this game, but for fans of the Super Smash Bros. series, it's great fun.

ESRB rating: T for Cartoon Violence, Crude Humor

games for the PS2 and PS3

LittleBigPlanet (LBP)

This award-winning game with a range of multi-player options centers around the creation of a virtual world in which objects work and behave as they do in real life. Players can share the worlds they create with others online.

ESRB rating: E for Comic Mischief, Mild Cartoon Violence

Race Driver: Grid

Gaming magazines have praised the special features of this racing game, including the Instant Replay and Flashback features. Several different track options from around the world and a choice of competitions (demolition derbies, GT races, and more) make this a great racing game for older kids.

ESRB rating: E

Buzz! Junior: Robo Jam

From the Buzz! Junior series, this title features a quirky collection of robot-themed mini-games that are easy to play using the Buzz! controllers. Families will love it.

ESRB rating: E for Comic Mischief, Mild Cartoon Violence

Hot Shots Golf: Out of Bounds

This fifth installment of the golfing game series is ideal for family play. Players initially can choose from six courses and fifteen players as they compete in virtual golf. Parents who've been trying to entice their reluctant kids onto the golf course may find the kids develop an interest after a few rounds of this game... Fore!

ESRB rating: E for Mild Suggestive Themes

TIDBIT: Almost $20 billion a year is spent on video game purchases.

Sega Superstars Tennis

Sonic the Hedgehog and other well-known video game characters (each with his own special skills) face off on the tennis courts. Play other family members or compete online with someone across the country!

ESRB Rating: E10+ for Mild Fantasy Violence, Mild Suggestive Themes, Mild Blood

Lego Indiana Jones: The Video Games

Experience your favorite parts of the Indiana Jones action movies in the form of a fedora-wearing Lego figure.

ESRB rating: E10+ for Cartoon Violence

Burnout Paradise

Race through Paradise City in this fast-paced game, often referred to as the king of arcade racing thanks to tight controls and an awe-inspiring sense of speed.

ESRB Rating: E10+ for Violence, Language

Buzz! The Hollywood Quiz

Test your Hollywood trivia knowledge with this great party game featuring more than 5,000 movie and celebrity questions, 100 movie clips, and more! Your teens will love it (and remember: There are many other Buzz! quiz games to try out!)!

ESRB Rating: T for Crude Humor, Drug Reference, Mild Language, Mild Violence, Suggestive Themes

TIDBIT: Although many of the Xbox titles are aimed at teens and young adults, the system does feature a wide range of parental control options. Parents can block games with certain ESRB ratings, as well as restrict the other players that kids compete with on Xbox Live. A timer option allows parents to pre-set how long their kids are allowed to be on the system on a daily or weekly basis.

Star Wars: The Force Unleashed

The latest Star Wars game allows players to move in the familiar intergalactic fantasy world, facing more than 50 enemies with various strengths and weaknesses. Star Wars enthusiasts will enjoy the new protagonist, Starkiller, Darth Vader's secret apprentice.

ESRB rating: T for Violence

games for
the xbox360

Rock Band

Up to four players perform in a virtual band using a microphone and different peripherals modeled after a guitar, bass guitar, and drum. Future rock stars play the "instruments" by reacting to scrolling on-screen notes. Fifty-eight songs are included; hundreds of songs are available to download.

ESRB rating: T for Lyrics, Mild Suggestive Themes

Guitar Hero

Players use guitar-shaped peripherals to re-create popular rock songs, following notes scrolling on-screen. Many versions of this game have been released since the 2005 original, including Guitar Hero World Tour which includes vocals and drums and Guitar Hero III: Legends of Rock, which exceeded $1 billion in sales.

ESRB rating: T for Lyrics, Mild Suggestive Themes

The Spiderwick Chronicles

Based on the popular children's books of the same name, this game features characters like Thimbletack, Jared, Simon, and Mallory, each of whom has a special weapon to fight off Mulgarath and protect Uncle Spiderwick and his book.

ESRB rating: E10+ for Animated Blood, Fantasy Violence

Dynasty Warriors 6

The latest Dynasty Warriors game allows players to swim across rivers and climb to higher positions as one of 41 different warriors fighting enemies in Ancient China. In the newest version, battlefields have been improved and enemies are able to adapt to attacks.

ESRB rating: T for Violence

Ghostbusters: The Video Game

Based on the film franchise and boasting a storyline by the writers of the film, Ghostbusters: The Video Game features many of the voices and likenesses of the original film actors. Players portray the team's new recruit investigating paranormal activity that seems to center around a new exhibit in the city.

ESRB rating: T for Comic Mischief, Fantasy Violence, Mild Language

MY STORY

"We have strict rules about 'screen time,' which refers to the time that the kids spend in front of the TV, video games, or computer. If they decide to play video games for the allotted two hours, they understand that they have given up all television and social networking for the rest of the day."

-*Michael, father of two*

Incredible Hulk

The Marvel Comics superhero is back! Bruce Banner and his green alter ego return for more global destruction.

ESRB rating: T for Mild Blood, Mild Language, Violence

Scene It? Lights, Camera, Action

Movie trivia entertainment comes to the Xbox 360 (thanks to the makers of the DVD-based board game) with four controllers so that the whole family can play. Gamers can battle for points or play in non-competitive party mode.

ESRB rating: T for Blood, Suggestive Themes, Use of Tobacco and Alcohol, Violence, Language

snack ideas for gamers

Gamers can work up quite an appetite so you'll want to have snacks available. You won't, however, want to put out anything that is likely to result in greasy hands or spills on controllers. Offer drinks in cans or boxes rather than glasses to minimize potential damage by enthusiastic players. Think neat finger foods, easy to grab between rounds.

Put out bowls of:

➡ Apple slices

➡ Pretzels

➡ Grapes

➡ Dry cereal like Kix, Fruit Loops, and Cheerios

➡ Yogurt or chocolate covered raisins

➡ Baby carrots

➡ Walnuts, pecans, or other less-greasy nuts

ideas for last minute family fun nights

Don't forgo Family Fun Night just because everyone is busy! Keep the tradition going with a quickie version of the event. Choose games that need no advance planning and can be played during dinner: You'll still have fun and no one will have to miss soccer practice or play rehearsal. Make a simple meal, grab take-out, or have food delivered. (Think beyond pizza and Chinese: Many traditional restaurants offer menu items to take out.)

Here are 18 terrific ideas for games your family can play without leaving the dinner table!

"What's under the napkin?"

1. Endless Order

One person starts out saying, "For dinner, I want a hot dog." The person next to her says, "For dinner, I want a hot dog and some green beans." The next person says, "For dinner, I want a hot dog, some green beans, and tater tots." Each person continues to repeat the list and add one item until someone gets it wrong and the game starts over.

2. What's Under the Napkin?

Hide something under your napkin while the others' eyes are closed. Who can guess what it is? (No touching!)

TIP: Three books that will turn dinnertime into game time

Zobmondo!! The Outrageous Book of Bizarre Choices

By Randy Horn. Would you rather...have regular encounters with aliens and not have proof OR have your best friend be invisible? Hundreds of "would-you-rather" questions will keep your dinner discussion interesting!

Can You Beat Ken?

Edited by Peter Crowell. This trivia book allows you to match wits with Ken Jennings, the all-time Jeopardy champ! It touts itself as "a book you can play!"

The Kids' Book of Questions

By Gregory Stock, Ph.D. The hundreds of questions posed in this book will provoke many interesting conversations!

3. Telephone with a Twist

Send two whispered messages in opposite directions around the table. The messages will criss-cross as they travel, making it doubly hard to remember the original sentences!

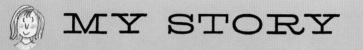

MY STORY

"We like to play a game called 'Roses and Thorns.' We go around the table and take turns talking about the best and worst things that have happened to us in the past week. Even on those weeks when I think I'm aware of everything's that happened, I'm always surprised by someone's story!"

-Christine, mother of three

4. Word of Mouth

Mouth a sentence to the person across from you; she has to guess what you said. No repeating the sentence!

5. Trivia Contest

Take turns posing questions to the group from Trivial Pursuit cards (disregard the game board and pie pieces). The youngest should have a chance to guess first.

6. Storyteller

Each person takes a turn grouping ten objects on the table and then choosing someone to make up a story that includes all ten objects. When the tale is over, the storyteller can put ten different objects on the table and choose someone else.

7. Family Trivia

Each person in turn asks the group a question about him or herself, such as: What game do I always play at recess? What is the first thing I do when I get to school/work? If I could do anything, what would I like to do on vacation? What was my happiest moment ever? What was my nickname when I was in first grade?

8. What's the Spoon Tapping?

Take turns hitting nearby items with your spoon while the others listen with their eyes closed and then offer guesses.

9. What's the Category?

Think of a category (things that are funny, things that you would find in Dad's closet...) and start listing items that would fall under the category. Who will guess that "car keys," "sunglasses," and "your mind" fall under the category of "things people in this family often lose"?

10. Indian Chief

While one person closes his eyes, the family selects someone to be the Indian Chief. When the person opens his eyes, the chief begins an action such as finger snapping, hand clapping, feet stomping, or fork tapping. The others immediately copy what he's doing. When he changes the action, the others follow. The person whose eyes were closed must guess who is playing the part of the chief. The chief for one round becomes the guesser for the next. Hint: The players must not watch the chief too closely or they will give him away!

TIDBIT: Wonder what benefits your kids are getting by playing games at the dinner table? A University of Michigan study found a strong link between regular family meal times and children's academic success and overall behavior. The largest study of teens found that those who had at least five dinners each week with a parent had higher grades and were less likely to engage in risky behavior than those who did not eat regularly with a parent.

11. Penny Slide

Take turns sliding pennies across the table, trying to get as close as possible to the target (the sugar bowl) without hitting it.

12. Mystery Adverb

While one person covers his ears, the others choose an adverb to describe how they will conduct themselves at the table— slowly, loudly, sadly, seriously... When the person removes his hands from his ears, he has one minute to watch how everyone behaves before he tries to guess the adverb. (Let him offer three guesses before he must give up.)

13. Never-ending Sentence or Never-ending Story

One person says the first word of a sentence or the first sentence of a story. The person next to her continues the sentence or the story. The game ends when the sentence gets ridiculously long or the story just gets ridiculous (and it will!).

14. Categories

"My friend Sam likes cookies, but not cake. He likes needles, but not thread. He loves doodling but hates drawing." Another person can chime in at any time: "Does he like bees but not wasps?" The first player would say, "Yes, he does" and the guesser would ask, "Is it because Sam likes things with double vowels?" The answer would be, "Yes!" The category can be as simple as things beginning with "c" or as tricky as "things you would find in a classroom."

15. What's Missing?

Remove something from the table while the others' eyes are closed. Who can guess what was removed?

16. Word Association

This is a silly game that requires little thought or concentration. One person says a word, any word, and the person next to her says the first word that comes to mind. The person next to her reacts to the second word and so on. The spoken words might go something like: car, plane, vacation, beach, bikinis…

MY STORY

"One of the greatest benefits we get from playing games at dinner time is that the kids tend to eat what's on their plate without dissecting and discussing everything. A few rounds of a trivia game and—what do you know!—everyone's green beans have disappeared!"

-Karen, mother of two

17. Three Strikes

One person begins the game by saying a letter. The next person offers up another letter, and must have a word in mind that begins with these two letters. The third person adds another letter, again with a word in mind. The object of the game is NOT to end the word, but to keep it going. Anyone who ends a word—even if it wasn't the one he had in mind—has a strike. If one player doesn't believe that another has a real word in mind, he can challenge and ask, "What's your word?" If the player does have a word, the challenger has a strike. If he doesn't have a word, he has a strike.

18. Who's Holding the Coin?

One person is designated the guesser. A coin is passed under the table from one person to another (excluding the guesser). At any point, the guesser can say, "Time!" and everyone must put their closed fists on the table. Can the guesser figure out who is holding the coin? If he's wrong, the person holding the coin can keep it. If he's right, he gets the coin and the person who had been holding it becomes the guesser.

TIP: Fill a basket on the dinner table with games for impromptu fun:

➡ Jump All But One triangle game with golf tees

➡ Mad Libs

➡ Trivia books and cards, such as the *Fact or Crap* cards

➡ Coffee stirrers to use as pick-up-sticks

➡ Dice for games like Farkel or Stack

➡ Rubik's cube

➡ Magnetic rocks

➡ Scrabble letters

➡ Blacksmith or tavern puzzles

➡ Dominoes

dinner ideas

If you're going to put together a quick meal rather than go the take-out route, you'll want to keep things as simple as possible so that you can get in on the dinnertime fun! Try our recipe for family-style nachos (and use paper plates to make clean-up super easy).

TIP: To find dinner recipes using only the food you have on hand, visit http://allrecipes.com. You can list the ingredients you want included (and those you don't) and the site will return a list of delicious ideas!

QUICK AND EASY
FAMILY NACHOS

Your family will love this "help yourself" plate of heaping nachos! You can alter the ingredients according to what you have in the refrigerator: use a different kind of cheese, substitute ground turkey for ground beef, or add the vegetable toppings that you have on hand. Make it simple!

Ingredients:

1 pound ground beef

1 ¼ ounce packet, taco seasoning mix

1 pound bag, tortilla chips

1 ½ cups shredded Mexican-style or cheddar cheese

2 cups shredded lettuce

2 tomatoes, chopped

1 onion, chopped

Salsa

Sour cream

Brown ground beef; drain fat.

Stir in taco seasoning and ¾ cup water. Bring to a boil, reduce heat, and simmer for 5 minutes. Stir frequently.

Spread chips onto a large, microwaveable platter and top with shredded cheese.

Microwave on high just until cheese begins to melt (or put on pizza pan in oven at 400 degrees until cheese melts).

Top with meat mixture, tomatoes, lettuce, onions, salsa, and sour cream.

Place in the center of the table and dig in!

CHAPTER THIRTEEN

read aloud family fun night

Reading books aloud to your children is a simple ritual that will help them establish a positive and lasting relationship with literature. When you read to kids, even for just 15 minutes at a time, you are helping to improve their vocabulary, inspire their imaginations, and enhance their listening skills.

TIP: When reading a book over the course of several weeks, always review what happened previously before you start reading again.

TIDBIT: The average reading speed is about 30 pages per hour. With this in mind, you can determine how long it will take to read a given book to your family.

Always begin by introducing the book: Read the title, subtitle, and the author's name. Mention any information that you think is important for an understanding of the story, and indicate the reasons you chose the book. You can decide whether it's best to share facts about the author or about specific events in the story (such as whether it's based on a true story) before or after you've finished the book. A bit of information piques curiosity; too much spoils the story!

TIP: The reader doesn't have to be a parent. An older sibling can read, or family members can pass the book around and take turns reading. If a book has lengthy sections of two-way dialogue, a parent can sit next to a child and they can read it together, essentially acting out the scene.

Read expressively with inflection and enthusiasm. Be animated! Allow your eyes and your voice to convey what's happening in the story. Pay close attention to what you're reading so that you know whether to raise or lower your voice, speed up or slow down, or speak in a higher or lower tone. Pause for dramatic effect. Differentiate among characters. All of these techniques help listeners engage in your story. If you read for more than about 20 minutes, allow the kids to ask questions or make comments as you go along. Also stop to explain words or ideas you think your kids might find confusing.

TIDBIT: Research conducted in the United Kingdom revealed that engaging in a simple task like doodling can keep people from daydreaming and thus improve their focus. Test subjects who doodled as they listened to a message had a 29 percent better recall of the specifics of the message than those who didn't doodle.

Children who are listening to a story might find their focus improves if they are involved in a simple activity such as drawing scenes they imagine from the book, playing with a stuffed animal (especially if the animal is represented in the story), knitting or crocheting, stacking blocks, or molding with Play Doh.

After you finish reading, engage the family in a discussion of the book. Even the youngest members of the family will be able to make worthwhile contributions to a literary dialogue if you ask the right questions!

The characters:

What did you think of ___? What did you like about him or her? What didn't you like? What are some words you would use to describe him or her: Brave? Cruel? Kind? Loyal? Greedy? Why did the character do the things s/he did? Would you have done the same things? Is this person like anyone you know? If you could be best friends with anyone in the book, who would it be? Why?

The plot or events of the story:

What was the most important thing that happened? What made that moment so important? What were you thinking when it happened? Did you expect it to happen or were you surprised? Was there anything you expected to happen that didn't?

The ending:

How do you feel about the way the story ended? If you could re-write this book, would you change the ending? If you would, how would you change it? Did anything about the ending surprise you? By the time the story ended, who learned or changed the most? Did you learn anything? Would you be interested to know what happens to the characters after the story ended?

In conclusion...

How would you describe this book to a friend? Would you want to read another book by the same author or about the same characters?

choosing a great book

You may think that your child's listening level (which is different from his reading level) is the most important factor to consider when selecting a read-aloud book. As important as that is, your own enthusiasm for the book is just as critical! In fact, your child would likely be engaged in a story that is a bit above his level if you read it with passion. Don't sacrifice your own reading pleasure!

When making a selection, look for books with engaging, well-paced storylines, as well as elements of suspense and adventure. For younger kids, you may initially want to read two or three shorter books by the same author. This will give them a sense of that author's voice but won't require them to stay focused for weeks at a time while you work through a longer novel.

 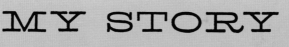

"Beware of beloved books from your own youth! I thought my kids would love a book called *Half Magic* as much as I did when I was young, but the dialogue was too antiquated and the story didn't move along quickly enough for them. I remembered it so differently! Some classics still work for kids today (mine did love *Pippi Longstocking*), but my advice for parents is to reassess them yourself before reading them to your kids."

-Mira, mother of two

You can opt for a nonfiction book if the entire family is interested in the topic: If, for example, you will be travelling to Ireland on your next vacation, you may be excited to learn about the country and its history. If you will be visiting the planetarium in a few weeks, you might find an interesting book on astronomy.

Be aware that there is a difference between a great book and a great read-aloud book. Books that you remember being among your favorites when you were younger might not work well in the read-aloud format. In addition, books with lengthy sections of descriptive passages are not as interesting to listen to as those with a lot of action. Extensive passages of dialogue make a book less than ideal, and it can be confusing unless the reader consistently uses different voices for each character.

You have access to great resources when you are choosing titles to read: your child's school librarian, your local public library's children's librarian, your child's teacher, and a number of read-aloud websites. Look for book bargains at your library's book sale, tag sales, used book stores, or book clubs through your children's schools. You can also trade books with other families.

MY STORY

"We established the 'two chapter rule' for books we read to the kids. Before giving a book I've chosen the thumbs down, the kids need to listen to at least two chapters. This gives them a bit of control, and yet forces them to give the book a chance before they reject it. So far, no vetoes! They have always wanted to hear more after the first two chapters."

-Mike, father of two

book ideas to get you started

With 170,000 new titles released every year, not to mention the books already lining the shelves of libraries and bookstores, compiling a comprehensive list of "must-reads" is nearly impossible. The lists that follow offer some family-friendly suggestions for books, book series, and authors. There are many, many more wonderful books that are not included in this brief overview, and some of the books here may not be suitable for your children. Consider this a place to begin your search for read-aloud books, but by no means a definitive resource.

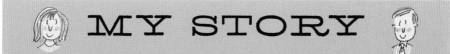

MY STORY

"We often start reading a book together, then finish it separately... one child might borrow it and read it for awhile, then pass it to another. Or we may do some reading to the younger kids while they're in the tub. The only rule is that when everyone has finished it, we all get together and discuss it."

-Colleen, mother of five

books to consider

My Father's Dragon
by Ruth Stiles Gannett (96 pages)

A simple, sweet tale that has been a favorite of youngsters since the 1940s, this book is perfect for kids who want to take part in reading to the family. Explore the other titles in the series: *The Dragons of Blueland* and *Elmer and the Dragon*.

TIP: For very young kids who enjoy picture books, you can combine an activity with the book for a complete Family Fun Night: *A House is a House for Me* (Mary Ann Hoberman) can inspire the kids to build their own houses out of large appliance boxes, for instance. *Snowy Day* (Ezra Jack Keats) can precede a snowflake-making craft. Websites for teachers or parents who home school can be great resources.

Falling Up
by Shel Silverstein (184 pages)

Poems are great for reading aloud, especially the humorous and often profound poems of Shel Silverstein. If your family enjoys the verses in this volume, try Silverstein's other collections: *A Light in the Attic* and *Where the Sidewalk Ends*.

Mr. Popper's Penguins
by Richard and Florence Atwater (139 pages)

This classic tale from 1938 follows the adventures of a housepainter, Mr. Popper, who dreams of polar exploration and unexpectedly receives a penguin as a gift. Though younger children will find it especially entertaining, parents will enjoy the story as well (and you may remember having it read to you many years ago)!

Alice in Wonderland
by Lewis Carroll (94 pages)

Not only is this work of literature a classic, but its episodic nature makes it perfect for reading aloud; you can share a few stories each week without worrying about playing catch-up with plots and characters. While kids will enjoy the fanciful stories and zany characters, older children and adults can ponder each story as an allegory.

Tuck Everlasting
by Natalie Babbitt (144 pages)

This short but engaging book prompts the question: If you could live forever, would you? When you've finished reading this book as a family, engage in a discussion about eternal life: If given the opportunity, would you drink from the fountain of youth?

MY STORY

"We formed a parent-child book club with other families in our neighborhood. We all read the same book aloud to our kids during the month and then get together for a discussion at someone's house. Knowing that we have that monthly meeting puts reading at the top of our priority list."

-Selena, mother of three

The Indian in the Cupboard
by Lynne Reid Banks (180 pages)

A rousing tale of toys coming to life combines fantasy with all the action you'd expect from a classic Western. Boys tend to love this book, as well as the other titles in the series.

The Cricket in Times Square
by George Selden (144 pages)

In a clever spin on the city mouse/country mouse tale, Chester Cricket from Connecticut inadvertently winds up at a Times Square newsstand in the company of Tucker Mouse and Harry Cat. Despite elegant new digs and fame as a celebrated musician, Chester misses his peaceful country life. Parents may remember reading this Newbery Award runner-up from 1961.

My Life in Dog Years
by Gary Paulsen (144 pages)

Each chapter of this heartwarming, nonfiction book works as a stand-alone story about a different dog that impacted the author's life, making it a great read-aloud for Family Fun Night. An ideal book for dog-loving families!

The Mouse and the Motorcycle
by Beverly Cleary (158 pages)

Of all the beloved characters Cleary has brought us, from Ramona the Pest to Henry Huggins, Ralph the Mouse is perhaps the most enduring (as well as endearing). Ralph's story, an engaging blend of fantasy and reality, offers just enough suspense and peril to engage (but not frighten) young readers.

Bridge to Terabithia
by Katherine Paterson (208 pages)

A timeless tale about the bonds of friendship and the power of imagination, Paterson's novel is perfect for families to enjoy together. A word of warning, though: It's a tear-jerker!

How to Eat Fried Worms
by Thomas Rockwell (128 pages)

A revolting classic since its original publication in 1973, *How to Eat Fried Worms* tells the story of Billy, who must eat 15 worms in 15 days in order to get money for a new minibike. The chants and rhymes about worm-eating make it fun to read aloud, especially to boys who will delight in every disgusting word!

Holes
by Louis Sachar (240 pages)

In this odd and oddly compelling Newbery Medal winner, Stanley Yelnats joins a group of other unfortunate boys at a juvenile detention facility known as Camp Green Lake. When Stanley discovers that there may be a sinister reason behind the holes they're forced to dig every day "to build character," the story becomes even more complex and bizarre (but also engrossing!).

Frindle
by Andrew Clements (112 pages)

Nick invents a new word and starts a battle with his teacher that is both hilarious and epic, eventually expanding to involve national publicity! This book about the power of language will be popular with everyone in the family.

TIP: If no one in the family is anxious to read aloud, check out the audio books section in your local library. You can listen to a family favorite on your CD player! Many libraries allow cardholders to download books onto their iPods or MP3 players for free.

You can also visit the iTunes home page and click on the bar about halfway down the right side of the screen that says "top audio books." There, you can see the top five best-selling audio books and can search for titles of interest to your family. Download a book and play it from your computer or put it on your iPod (you can then connect your iPod to a set of speakers so the whole family can enjoy the book).

The Slave Dancer
by Paula Fox (192 pages)

In this work of historical fiction, a young boy is kidnapped and forced to play music aboard a slave ship so that the slaves will dance, keeping them healthy and strong during the voyage. This easy-to-follow journey tale has characters so appealing your family will be engrossed from beginning to end.

My Side of the Mountain
by Jean Craighead George (192 pages)

Young Sam Gribley runs away from home to the Catskill Mountains, where he spends a year living in a hollowed-out tree with a falcon and a weasel for friends. His desire for freedom is stronger than the loneliness and harsh weather he's forced to battle. If your family enjoys this book, check out the more than 80 other titles by the same author.

The Hobbit
by J.R.R. Tolkein (320 pages)

When Gandalf the Grey comes calling, Bilbo Baggins is pulled into a dangerous adventure that will change him forever. This fantasy classic appeals especially to boys, and its episodic nature makes it easy to pick up and put down over the course of several weeks.

The Swiss Family Robinson
by Johann D. Wyss (352 pages)

Considering that this book was written nearly 200 years ago, it is still a compelling family read. When a ship is thrown off course by a storm, a Swiss man, his wife, and four sons are shipwrecked on a tropical island. Their struggles to survive and the ingenuity they exhibit make this an enduring adventure tale.

our favorite books to read as a family are:

book series to consider

The Little House on the Prairie series
by Laura Ingalls Wilder

The nine titles in this series follow Laura's life in the late 1800s, from her childhood in the Big Woods of Wisconsin to her life with husband Almanzo on their prairie homestead. Young girls, particularly, will love hearing about Laura's adventures, and adults will enjoy reflecting on a simpler time. (It's especially fun to read *The Long Winter* on a cold January day to remind the kids just how much times have changed!)

The Harry Potter series
by J.K. Rowling

Dive into the series that has become a cultural phenomenon! The first book is 320 pages long; the other six get progressively longer. You may want to rent the movie versions of the books after you've read them for a comparison. (If the page count is a little daunting, check out the audio version of the book, which has gotten rave reviews.)

The Magic Tree House series

by Mary Pope Osborne

When Jack and Annie discover a magic tree house in the woods, they are pulled into a series of adventures that take them from the Cretaceous period to ancient Egypt to France in the middle ages. Kids can read one of these books aloud to the rest of the family (they run 60 pages and up), and everyone will take away a tidbit or two of historical information.

 MY STORY

"Even though using television to promote reading might seem counterproductive, the PBS show Reading Rainbow really turned my kids on to books. It's a show worth looking into!"

-Fiona, mother of three

A Series of Unfortunate Events

by Lemony Snicket

This quirky series of thirteen books—in turn funny, frightening, and truly odd—makes for interesting family reading. Starting with *The Bad Beginning* and finishing, appropriately, with *The End*, you'll follow the zany adventures of the Baudelaire orphans as they work themselves out of one predicament only to fall into another. The author pitched the concept to his publisher by saying that this is what he would have wanted to read as a ten-year-old boy.

authors to consider

MARK TWAIN, aka Samuel Clemens, was a humorist and writer whose books are as appealing today as when he wrote them in the mid to late 1800s. *The Adventures of Huckleberry Finn* is considered a masterpiece of American fiction; *The Adventures of Tom Sawyer* and *A Connecticut Yankee in King Arthur's Court* were well received when they were published, earning Twain a worldwide audience, and these titles are still popular today. The timeless humor will appeal to the whole family and, because his works are episodic (each chapter contains an individual episode in the overall story), they are perfect to read aloud over the course of several Family Fun Nights.

SID FLEISCHMAN is the Newbery Award-winning author of *The Whipping Boy* and nearly 60 other outstanding books for young readers. He initially wanted to be a magician, which likely led him to write *Mr. Mysterious and Company*. The concept for his well-known book *The Ghost in the Noonday Sun* came from folklore that told of the ability of those who were born at midnight to see ghosts. Other titles include *Jim Ugly, Humbug Mountain, Bandit's Moon*, and *By The Great Horn Spoon!* If your family takes an interest in Fleischman, read *The Abracadabra Kid: A Writer's Life*, which is his autobiography (with his tips for becoming a writer).

JANE YOLEN has written or edited almost three hundred books, many of them award-winners, ranging from the *Commander Toad* series to the *Pit Dragon* trilogy. She has been referred to as the "Hans Christian Andersen of America" and "a modern equivalent of Aesop." Yolen's masterpieces include the *Young Merlin* trilogy, *The Devil's Arithmetic, Sleeping Ugly, Briar Rose*, and *The Dragon's Boy*.

ROALD DAHL wrote wonderful read-aloud books for children with quirky characters and zany plot twists, often told from the child's point of view. Many of his books appear to reflect his own unpleasant early years in boarding schools. His humor is a bit dark and his books do feature some rather grotesque scenes such as those in *The Witches* and *George's Marvelous Medicine*, but these techniques make his books edgy enough to appeal to audiences of all ages. He is probably best known for *James and the Giant Peach, Charlie and the Chocolate Factory* and *Matilda*, a great book for girls about the power of knowledge and the love of reading. *The Twits*, at just 96 pages, might be a good first choice for a read-aloud book.

AVI was told by teachers from the time he was young that his writing made no sense; at the time, no one realized that he had a learning disability. A devoted tutor began working with him and he continued writing; today he is a prize-winning author of dozens of popular books for children and young adults. *The True Confessions of Charlotte Doyle* (especially popular with girls), *Midnight Magic, Crispin: The Cross of Lead, Poppy, Strange Happenings, The Seer of Shadows*, and *The Good Dog* are among his best.

JERRY SPINELLI, author of 25 books, is best known for his novels about early adolescence like *Maniac Magee* (winner of the 1991 Newbery medal), *Wringer* (a 1998 Newbery Honor book), and *Space Station Seventh Grade*. His books have special appeal for the 9 to 12 age group. Other Spinelli titles include *Milkweed, Eggs, Stargirl, There's a Girl in My Hammerlock*, and *Loser*.

 # MY STORY

"My kids range in age from 4 to 17, so reading aloud wouldn't work for us. Instead, we have a weekly reading night where everyone brings his own book to read to himself in the living room. We play music quietly in the background and, if it's cold enough, we'll light a fire in the fireplace."

-L'Tonya, mother of three

food for thought

Many family-friendly books have multiple references to food—some serious, some silly. It's always fun to plan a meal around the theme of a book you're reading together. Some books make it easy with companion cookbooks: *The Little House on the Prairie* series, for instance, includes a cookbook called *The Little House Cookbook* (by Barbara M. Walker) that features more than one hundred frontier recipes from the classic stories. If you're reading *Charlie and the Chocolate Factory* or *James and the Giant Peach*, check out *Roald Dahl's Revolting Recipes* (by Josie Fision and Felicity Dahl). Amy Cotler has written *The Secret Garden Cookbook: Recipes Inspired by Frances Hodgson Burnett's The Secret Garden*. For a comprehensive list of literature-inspired cookbooks, visit http://www.scils.rutgers.edu/professional-development/childlit/ChildrenLit/cookbooks.html.

If the book you're reading doesn't have a cookbook associated with it, search the Internet for recipes that would complement the topic, historical period, or geographic location of your title.

TIP: Conventional publishing wisdom says that girls don't mind reading books with a boy as the main character, but boys don't like to read books with a girl protagonist. In addition, publishers believe that kids prefer to read books about kids who are older than they are. The exception to this is when the young age of the main character makes him or her especially funny, like Beverly Cleary's "Ramona."

TIP: Parents' recommendations

Brenda, mother of two: "Bruce Coville's books."

Lisa, mother of two: "*Sarah, Plain and Tall* and *Molly's Pilgrim*, favorites of my girls."

Mark, father of three: "*Curse of the Ruins,* by Gary Paulsen."

Chris, mother of three: "*Anne of Green Gables*, especially for girls."

Alex, mother of one: "Books by Natalie Babbitt."

Kate, mother of one: "The *American Girl* series of books that complement the dolls."

Corinne, mother of two: "*The Best Christmas Pageant Ever* and other books in the same series."

Mary, mother of four: "*The Spiderwick Chronicles*: Boys love them."

Sandi, mother of two: "*The Railway Children*, even though the book is a century old!"

Carin, mother of three: "Just about anything by Andrew Clements."

Nick, father of two: "The *Narnia* series by C.S. Lewis."

Camara, mother of one: "Anything that Michael Doris wrote for kids."

CHAPTER FOURTEEN

ideas for thrifty family fun nights

You don't have to spend a lot of money to have a terrific time with your family. In fact, sometimes the best and most memorable activities are ones that cost next to nothing. The ideas outlined in this chapter may require an investment of your time, but they won't require you to open your wallet. (The change in your pocket should suffice.)

TIDBIT: According to the most recent data from the Bureau of Labor Statistics, the average American family spends about $2,500 each year on entertainment and recreation. Of course, this figure increases with larger families. That's quite a chunk of your family's annual budget!

here are 10 family fun nights that cost less than $10 each!

1. Family Olympics:

Your family can set up an Olympics-style competition that will challenge young and old alike! The key is to come up with a series of events that create a level playing field so that age as well as physical size and strength are not necessarily advantages. Some ideas for "Olympic" events are:

LONGEST FLIGHT: Everyone has five minutes to make a paper airplane, after which the competitors line up and prepare to throw their creations. The person whose plane flies the greatest distance wins.

FIRST BUBBLE: Hand everybody a piece of bubble gum and tell them to start chewing. Who will be the first one to make a bubble larger than two inches across?

HOOPS: Everyone gets 10 pairs of rolled-up socks and stands the same distance away from an empty wastebasket. Who can make the greatest number of baskets?

WORD SEARCH: Each person has three minutes to find the most words within the phrase "Family Fun Night." Kids can make two and three letter words; adults' words must have at least four letters.

WOOZY WALK: Spin players around five times and then have them try to walk along a straight line you've laid on the ground with a piece of masking tape. Who can stay on the line?

2. Personal Pictionary

Make your own Pictionary-type game! In advance, a parent can write or type words on slips of paper, fold each one, and put them all in a jar. When it's time to play, each person can take a turn choosing a word and drawing a picture of it while the others try to guess what she is drawing. If someone guesses correctly, he and the artist each get one point.

TIP: Check out www.gamedaze.com and click on "Games Under $10." You'll find Clue, Candyland, Checkers, dominoes, dice and card games, and more!

3. Science Experiments

You and your kids can conduct fascinating scientific research with objects you have around the house. A number of excellent books and websites can provide detailed information. To get started, try these three experiments:

EXPLODING COLORS: Pour just enough milk into a pizza pan or baking dish to cover the bottom. Add a few drops of food coloring to the milk in the center of the pan. Squeeze two or three drops of dish detergent on top of the food coloring and watch the fireworks! Read about hydrophobic molecules to find out what happened.

ROCKET LAUNCHER: Pour ½ cup of water and ½ cup of vinegar into a one-quart soda bottle. Put 1 teaspoon of baking soda in the middle of a 4⊠ x 4⊠ piece of paper towel and twist the ends together to keep the baking soda in place. Once outside, push the paper towel full of baking soda into the bottle and press on a cork top. (You can use a tack to attach streamers to the cork for added effect!) Stand back: The baking soda will react with the vinegar and the cork will shoot into the air! Read about carbon dioxide gas to find out what happened.

BOTTLED EGG: Find a glass bottle with an opening that is slightly smaller than an egg. Drop a small piece of paper and a lit match into the bottle. Immediately place a hard-boiled egg (with no shell) on top of the bottle, covering the opening. Even though it is larger than the opening, the egg will drop into the bottle! Read about vacuums and high and low air pressure to find out what happened.

4. Puzzle Race

If you think that doing puzzles is too tame, try this twist! Each member of the family chooses a puzzle. (If you don't have enough for everyone, puzzles can be purchased at your local dollar store for—you guessed it—one dollar.) Dump all of the puzzle pieces into a pile, mix them up, then… BEGIN! Who can find all the right pieces and finish his or her puzzle first?

TIP: Peruse a thrift store for games that can be played whether all the pieces are in the box or not. Trivial Pursuit cards, for instance, can be used without the game board. Collect cards, dice, playing pieces, spinners, and timers to create your own one-of-a-kind game.

5. Spit-It-Out Trivia Contest

You'll laugh your way through this trivia game, win or lose! In advance, make a list of trivia questions and answers (from the Internet, game cards, or books). At game time, divide the family into teams of two: partners will take turns asking and answering the questions. Each team has one minute to get as many right answers as possible. Here's the catch: Place a bowl of Saltines or Ritz crackers in the middle of the table. Every time a teammate answers a question correctly, the player posing the questions must eat a cracker. By the time a player is asking his tenth question, his partner can barely understand what he is saying!

MY STORY

"My son loves to take photos, and he created a great game for our family to play. He takes close-up shots of all sorts of things around the house. Once a month or so, he prints them out and hangs them up on the kitchen bulletin board. We all try to identify the photos. It's a lot harder than you'd think!"

-Zoe, mother of four

6. Make-Your-Own Mad Libs

Mad Libs are funny enough on their own, but when you take the time to create personal stories for your own family, you'll never stop laughing! Study a few Mad Libs to see how they're written, then write your own unique stories and have your family members fill in the blanks!

7. Balloon Football

If your group is looking for a little more action on Family Fun Night, play a gentle version of football. Divide your group into two teams and line up about 30 feet from one another. Each team should position a goalie behind the opposing team who must remain standing on a chair holding a pin throughout the game. Each team tries to hit the balloon toward its own goalie so that the goalie can pop the balloon and score a point for his team. At the same time, the opposing team tries to prevent the point from being scored. The balloon must stay in the air at all times. Note: Have plenty of balloons on hand!

TIP: Make your own Bingo game and use the dollar store or garage sales as sources for prizes. For instructions on making your own game, visit www.brownielocks.com/bingo.html.

8. Game of Giants

Make your own game board by placing old magazines on the floor in two rows of ten "spaces" (marked by magazines) each. Divide the family into teams and come up with a game token for each team (such as a stuffed animal). Using two sets of trivia cards, one for kids and one for adults, take turns asking and answering questions. A team moves ahead one giant space for each correct answer!

9. Soda Bottle Bowling

Pour a few inches of water into (and then cap) a set of 2-liter soda bottles; set them up like bowling pins. Take turns kicking a soccer ball into the pins to see who can knock down the most.

 # MY STORY

"We play a tabletop version of shuffleboard that the kids love. I use painter's tape to create a shuffleboard triangle on the dining room table. We use the caps off of milk or water bottles to slide across the table the way you would slide traditional shuffleboard pieces, and we play and score by the same rules. A taste of retirement living in our own kitchen!"

-Charlie, father of three

10. Wacky Story Time

Give everyone a piece of paper and a pen, and instruct them to write the first sentence of a story. When you say "now," each person folds the paper back so that what he wrote is hidden, and passes it to the person on his right. Then, each person writes the next sentence of his story and at "now," folds and passes the paper again. Everyone is writing a continuation of his own story, but on a different piece of paper each time. After a pre-established number of passes, everyone reads aloud the story on the paper he is holding, connecting the sentences as naturally as possible.

TIP: Ask older relatives what they did for fun when they were young. You'll get some great ideas for thrifty activities!

"There once was a monster who loved marshmallows.
As she got into bed, she heard a noise.
INSPECTOR MOUSTACHE CLIMBED OUT OF A HOLE..."

cheap eats

You can put together a delicious Family Fun Night dinner using food you already have in the refrigerator and the pantry. Here are two budget-friendly recipes sure to please your brood.

 ## MY STORY

"It's such a special treat for my two girls when we set up our own 'family restaurant.' We take out the good china and the linen tablecloth and napkins, light candles, play soft music, and we dress up. We serve the same food we always do, but the fact that it's served in a fancy way makes it special!"

-Hannah, mother of two

STIR-FRY DINNER

This flexible stir-fry recipe uses up the leftovers in the fridge, making use of whatever you have on hand and requiring few, if any, extra purchases at the grocery store.

Ingredients:

2 tablespoons vegetable oil, divided

1 pound meat or meat substitute (choose one or more from list below)

1 onion, chopped

1 clove garlic, minced

1 teaspoon ginger

4 cups vegetables (choose three or more from list below)

½ cup broth (chicken, beef, or vegetable)

2 tablespoons soy sauce

2 teaspoons cornstarch

½ cup extra ingredient (choose one from list below)

MEAT CHOICES: Boneless chicken strips, boneless beef stir-fry strips, boneless pork strips, raw shrimp, tofu cubes

VEGETABLE CHOICES: Pepper strips, mushroom slices, celery pieces, snow peas, zucchini slices, carrot slices, broccoli florets

EXTRA INGREDIENTS: Nuts, sesame seeds, crispy Chinese noodles, crispy fried onion bits

Heat 1 tablespoon of oil over high heat. Add meat and stir-fry until just cooked through. Set meat aside.

Heat remaining tablespoon of oil in pan; add onion, garlic, and ginger. Cook for 1 minute. Add vegetable choices and cook for another 2 minutes.

Add the broth to the vegetables, cover, and let steam for 2 or 3 minutes.

Meanwhile, in a small bowl, stir together soy sauce and cornstarch.

When vegetables are tender, add the meat and soy sauce mixture to the pan. Stir-fry for another 1 to 2 minutes or until the sauce is thickened.

Remove from heat and sprinkle with the extra ingredient. Serve over rice.

MAKE-YOUR-OWN
ICE CREAM

Each person in the family can make his very own ice cream—in a bag! The only thing you may need to buy is half-and-half.

Ingredients (for a single serving):

2 tablespoons sugar

1 cup half and half

½ tsp vanilla

Additional supplies needed:

½ cup of salt

Ice cubes

Small and large re-sealable plastic bags

Fill the large plastic bag halfway with ice cubes; add ½ cup of salt.

Fill the smaller bag with sugar, half-and-half, and vanilla. Seal it shut and place it inside the larger bag, then seal the larger bag.

Shake the bag until the mixture hardens (about 5 minutes).

Dump the ice cream from the small bag into a bowl and enjoy!

CHAPTER FIFTEEN

card sharks night

Historians can trace playing cards back to the 10th century, when the Chinese began using paper dominoes the way we use cards today. There are also indications that Chinese gamblers at that time used actual paper money as cards, playing with and for the money. No one knows how and when cards made their way to Europe, although by the mid 15th century, historians note references to playing cards in England. During the reign of Edward IV, cards were allowed to be played only during the 12 days of Christmas!

TIDBIT: In the United States, the backs of playing cards were plain until the 1850s.

TIDBIT: Over the years, there were many different suit symbols used. Before the traditional hearts, spades, clubs, and diamonds were established, symbols like wine pots, books, cups, and a variety of animals appeared on cards.

Fortunately, for us, playing cards is a lawful, year-round pastime. Popular with multiple generations, card games are perfect for Family Fun Night. Games like Seven Card Stud are especially appealing to teens, and they will help entice them to stay home on a Friday night. There are hundreds of terrific family games; just a handful of favorites are described here to get you started, with the easiest games listed first. A number of books and reliable websites can provide more extensive information. A good resource is www.pagat.com, which gives the rules for card games popular here and in other parts of the world.

TIDBIT: The Joker was added to the familiar 52-card deck sometime in the 1860s because players felt that an extra trump card was needed.

TIDBIT: Packs of playing cards in Italy, Spain, Germany, and Switzerland do not have Queens.

slapjack

Anyone who can recognize the Jack can play this fast-paced game.

What you need:

Standard deck of cards

2 to 4 players

Goal:

To win all the cards in the deck

How to play:

The dealer shuffles and deals the entire deck of cards face down. Players may not look at their cards but should tap them into a neat pile.

Moving quickly, each player in turn takes the top card from his pile and slaps it face up in the center of the table. When the card is a Jack, every player tries to slap his hand on top of it. The first to put his hand on the Jack wins the entire pile of cards. The winning player shuffles the new cards into his existing pile. Play continues.

If anyone mistakenly slaps a card that is not a Jack, he must give the top card from his pile to the player whose card he slapped.

Players who run out of cards are out; the game continues until someone wins all of the cards.

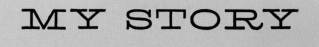
"We play cards for pennies, rocks, jellybeans—even seashells (when we were on vacation at the beach)! We have a jar in the kitchen where we toss our pennies so that we have enough to play with on our family card nights."

-Steve, father of four

TIP: Many websites, including www.expertvillage.com, feature video series to teach viewers a variety of ways to shuffle cards. Log on and learn!

spoons

Few card games serve up the kind of excitement that Spoons does!

What you need:

Standard deck of cards

Spoons (one fewer than the number of players)

3 or more players

Goal:

To collect four cards of one kind and to avoid being the one without a spoon

How to play:

To begin, place the spoons (one fewer than the number of players) in the center of the table within reach of all players. Four cards of one rank are required for each player, meaning that if you have just four players, you'll use just the Aces, Kings, Queens, and Jacks. Once the dealer has chosen the cards to be used, she shuffles them and deals out four to each player.

When the dealer says, "Pass," players simultaneously discard one card face down to their left and pick up the card that the player on their right has discarded. Play continues this way, as quickly as possible, until someone collects four of a kind. When this happens, he takes a spoon: He can grab it or quietly sneak it. As soon as other players notice, they must all grab for spoons. The player left without a spoon loses the round and is given the letter "S," the first letter in "SPOONS." When a player has amassed enough letters to spell out the word, she's out.

The player left at the end is the winner.

(If grabbing for spoons is too aggressive, a player who finds he has four of a kind can place his finger on his nose; the last one to copy his action is out.)

match up

This simple game is great for kids who are new to cards because they must learn to recognize suits.

What you need:

Standard deck of cards (Ace is high)

2 or more players

Goal:

To be the first player to get rid of all of your cards

How to play:

The dealer shuffles and deals seven cards to each player; the rest are placed facedown in the middle of the table as stock cards. Players may look at the cards they were dealt.

The player to the dealer's right places any card from his hand face up on the table. In turn, players must place a card on the previous one that matches its suit or number. For example, if a player puts down a three of clubs, the next player must play either a three or any clubs. If he doesn't have an appropriate card, he must draw from the stockpile until he finds a suitable card. If he takes every card in the pile and still doesn't get one that is the right number or suit, he passes and the next player continues. When every player has played all his cards or passed, the one who played the last card must play a new card to start a new round.

The first player to put down all of his cards wins.

liar, liar

You may recognize this as a family-friendly version of the game "B.S."

What you need:

Standard deck of cards (Ace is low)

2 to 5 players

Goal:

To be the first player to get rid of all of your cards

How to play:

The dealer shuffles and deals the entire deck. Players may look at and organize their cards.

One player (usually the one to the left of the dealer) begins by placing between one and four Aces face down in the center of the table, saying aloud the number of cards he is putting down, such as, "Three Aces." The player to his left must place from one to four twos face down, again, announcing it out loud, and the next player, threes, and so on. The cards must be in sequence.

Here's the catch: Because the cards are being placed face down, players don't have to play the cards they are reporting. If a player doesn't have the card that is supposed to be played, for example a six, she can bluff by putting down a three and calling out, "One six."

After each turn, anyone who suspects that the last player was bluffing can say, "Liar, Liar!" and turn over the card in question. If the player was bluffing (for example, he called out, "Two threes!" but instead played two Kings), he must add the entire pile of cards to his hand. If he did not lie, however, and the cards he put down were the ones he announced, then the player who called his bluff by shouting "Liar, Liar!" must add the entire pile to her hand!

The first player to run out of cards wins.

president

You can simplify this game by removing the hierarchy and following the basic rules, playing as many rounds as time permits.

What you need:

Standard deck of cards (Ace is high)

3 or more players

Goal:

To be the first player to get rid of all of your cards

How to play:

The dealer shuffles and deals the entire deck to the players. (It doesn't matter if the hands aren't perfectly even.) Players may look at the cards in their hands.

The player to the left of the dealer places a card in the middle of the table. Play continues to the left, with each player putting down a card that is equal or higher in rank to the previous one. If the first player plays doubles or triples (meaning two or three cards of the same rank), all subsequent players must play doubles or triples. Players cannot play doubles or triples unless the first player started the round with doubles or triples.

If a player cannot put down a card that is equal to or higher than the previous card, he must pass. Players can also choose to pass if they do not want to play their cards at that time. If every player passes, then the pile is cleared and the person who played the last card starts the next round with any card or cards (typically a lower card, because they're more difficult to get rid of).

Game play continues until one player runs out of cards. He wins the round and is declared the President (see "hierarchy").

Special rules:

SKIPPING: If someone plays the same card on top of what was just played (for example, if a player plays an Ace and the next player also puts down an Ace), the next player skips his turn.

SOCIALS: If a player plays one, two, or three cards of a certain rank and another player has the remaining one, two, or three cards of that rank in her hand, she can play all of them immediately (even if it isn't her turn) by shouting "Social" before another player has a chance to make a play. The player who uses a "Social" may then put down any card she desires to begin the round again.

TWOS: Twos can be used to clear the pile. The player who uses the two can then start the round with any card or cards in her hand.

Hierarchy:

The winner of each round is declared the President and the loser of each round is declared an Average Joe. When the next hand is dealt, the Average Joe must give his best card to the President, and the President gives her worst card to the Average Joe. The President then starts the new round. For added fun, your family could allow the President of each round to sit in a special chair (or offer up another fun perk), because there will likely be a different President after each round.

black lady hearts

This classic card game can also be fun to play in teams! In a group of 4 or 6, the player sitting across from you becomes your team member, and the two of you combine your scores at the end of each round.

What you need:

Standard deck of cards (Ace is high)

Pencil and paper to keep score

2 to 6 players (4 is ideal)

Goal:

To avoid the Queen of Spades and all heart cards, or to "shoot to the moon" by taking every heart card and the Queen of Spades

How to play:

The dealer shuffles and then deals the entire deck evenly among all players. If it's not possible for players to end up with exactly the same number of cards, remove several of the lowest cards from the deck. Choose one player to keep score.

At the start of each round (the rounds are called "tricks" and consist of each player, in turn, playing one card), players look at their cards and pass three cards of their choosing to the player on the left. (Players generally give away the highest cards in their decks). The player to the left of the dealer begins by playing any card in his deck (except for hearts) face up in the center of the table. In succession, each player must play a card of the same suit. If a player does not have a card of the same suit, she can play any card that she'd like to play, even a heart. Once a heart is played on a different suit (meaning that a suit other than a heart started the trick), players can then begin tricks with hearts. If players find this rule confusing, it can be disregarded and players can start tricks with hearts as they choose.

After each person has played one card, the player who played the highest card in the suit that led wins the trick. Note that winning the trick is not always a good thing (see scoring below for details); players want to avoid winning tricks containing heart cards and the Queen of Spades. The player who won the trick starts the next trick by playing any card in his deck. The cards that he won in the previous trick are not added to his hand but placed aside for scoring at the end of the round.

Game play continues until all players are out of cards, ending the first round. Game play continues with subsequent rounds in this manner until one player reaches a previously determined score (50, 75, or 100 points). The player with the lowest score at that point wins, and the highest score loses.

Scoring:

1 point for each heart card won in a trick

13 points if a player wins the Queen of Spades

SHOOTING THE MOON: If a player wins all 13 hearts and the Queen of Spades, 26 points are deducted from his score, and 26 points are added to the scores of every other player!

Extra scoring options:

Deduct 10 points for the Jack of Diamonds

ALTERNATE SCORING: Ace of Hearts is 14 points, King of Hearts is 13 points, Queen of Hearts is 12 points, Jack of Hearts is 11 points, ten of hearts is 10 points, nine of hearts is 9 points, and so on. Queen of Spades is 50 points and Jack of Diamonds is negative 40 points. Games continue to 250, 275, or 300 points. "Shooting the Moon" scoring changes, too, with 100 points deducted from the player's score, and 100 points added to the scores of every other player!

TIP: Five fun family games you already know how to play

→ Go Fish

→ War

→ Old Maid

→ Concentration

→ Crazy Eights

OLD MAID

TIDBIT: Building a house of cards

Bryan Berg, who holds the Guinness World Record for building the largest house of cards, travels all over the world showing off his special talent. He built a 14-foot tall house in the shape of Cinderella's Castle using 3,000 decks of cards, and he spent 20 days in Hong Kong just before the Beijing Olympics building the Athlete Village in cards. He used 50,000 cards to build a replica of Gotham City in Antwerp to celebrate *The Dark Knight*. You can check out his work at his website: www.cardstacker.com.

Building a house of cards is best suited for family members with a great deal of patience, an artistic vision, and most importantly, a steady hand. Here's a tip from the experts: Old, worn-out cards are better for building than newer cards, which tend to be slick. And, unlike Bryan, you'll probably want to start out using just one deck!

poker games

Poker games are great for pre-teens and teens, who always have to assess the "cool" factor before committing to a family activity.

MY STORY

"We use chocolate coins for betting when we play poker and the kids couldn't be happier about it. I mean, candy and money all in one? C'mon!"

-Leslie, mother of two

betting terms for poker

Call: Place a bid that equals the previous bid.

Raise: Place a bid that equals the previous bid plus as many additional tokens as the player is willing to risk. (Subsequent bidders must then meet this raised bid.)

Fold: Drop out. The player gives up and automatically loses the round.

In a standard Poker game, two or more players are required, a standard deck of cards is used (Ace is high), and tokens such as coins or Skittles are needed. The goal of any poker game is to get the best hand and win the pot (or to bluff and trick all of the other players into folding in order to win the pot).

TIP: Everyone has a particular betting pattern. If you can figure out what it is, you have a much better chance of winning! Does the player on your left get talkative when he has a good hand? Does the one across the table always raise when he has a great hand? People tend to be very consistent, so pay close attention to patterns and use them to your advantage!

Given this tip, make sure that none of the other players can recognize your betting pattern! Change it up a bit so that you remain a bit of a mystery.

scoring

(the following are ranked highest to lowest):

Royal Straight Flush: Ace-King-Queen-Jack-10

Straight Flush: Five cards in sequence of the same suit

Four of a Kind: Four cards of the same rank

Full House: Three of a kind and one pair (between two or more hands, the highest card in the "three of a kind" wins)

Flush: Five cards of the same suit

Straight: Five cards in sequence, not the same suit

Three of a Kind: Three cards of the same rank

Two Pair: Two matches (two cards of one rank, two cards of another rank)

One Pair: One match (two cards of the same rank)

High Card: Highest-ranked card in the hand

Note: Between two or more hands with the same score (for example, two players have a straight), the player with the highest card wins.

blind man's bluff

This silly, basic version of poker is great for younger kids, and it's also a perfect way to introduce your family to more complex casino games because the basics of betting and perfecting your "poker face" are presented in an entertaining way.

What you need:

Standard deck of cards (Ace is high)

Tokens, such as chips or candy

2 or more players

Goal:

To have the highest card and win the pot

How to play:

The dealer shuffles the deck and deals one card face down to each player. The players are not permitted to look at their cards.

The round begins when each player antes up, placing one token in the center of the play area. (Even if a player plans to fold immediately, he must ante up at the beginning of the round.) Each player holds her card on her forehead with one hand during game play so that players can see one another's cards, but cannot see their own cards. If a player looks at his own card, he's out automatically.

Game play begins with the player to the left of the dealer. He looks around the table to determine his chances of having the highest card at the table. The player then has two options: He can place a bid by adding any number of his tokens to the pot (the center of the game play area), or he can fold. Each subsequent player can either call or raise the bid.

Once all bets are in, players remove the cards from their foreheads and compare. High card takes the pot; a tie splits the pot. The dealer deals a new card to each player from the remaining deck. Game play continues until there are no cards remaining in the deck.

blackjack

You'll feel like you're in Vegas as you mentally add up your cards and decide whether or not to take a chance on hitting 21!

What you need:

Standard deck of cards (Ace is high)

Tokens, such as chips or candy

2 or more players

Goal:

To get a hand that adds up to 21 (or comes as close as possible to 21 without exceeding it)

How to play:

The dealer gives each player two cards: One is placed face up and the other is placed face down.

Each player looks at his facedown card and mentally calculates the sum of the two. (Aces are worth 11, face cards are worth 10, and all other cards are worth their face value.) Players then bet a certain number of their tokens based on how confident they are that their cards combined are close to 21. (Your family can decide whether each player can bet any number of his tokens or if more regimented betting rules should be employed.)

The player to the left of the dealer begins. She can say, "Stick" to the dealer if she does not want any more cards. She can say, "Hit me" if she wants one more card, face up, to get her total closer to 21. She can say, "Hit me" as many times as she'd like until she decides to say, "Stick." But beware: As soon as her score exceeds 21, she is "busted," meaning that she is out.

Play continues in this manner until all players are either "stuck" or "busted." At that point, all players' cards are revealed. The player whose cards are closest to 21 wins all of the tokens that were bet. A tie splits the pot. (Note: An Ace combined with a black Jack automatically trumps all other combinations of cards.)

TIP: Bluffing is an essential skill for poker, because it allows you to win with an inferior hand. Bluffing takes advantage of the fact that poker is a game of incomplete information: Just by acting as if you have a great hand and getting others to believe you, you can win!

But you have to be smart about bluffing: It doesn't matter how often you bluff, it matters how often your bluffing works. Bluff when you are in a late position and no one before you has shown a strong hand, when your cards that are showing make it possible that you have a strong hand, when you sense other players will fold to a bet, or when you have only one opponent.

five card draw

The rules for Five Card Draw are easy to follow, making it one of the first poker games many people learn to play.

What you need:

Standard deck of cards (Ace is high)

Tokens, such as chips or candy

2 or more players

Goal:

To get the high hand

How to play:

Players ante up. The dealer deals five cards down to each player. Players look at their own hands.

Bets are placed after the initial deal. After the betting round, each player may exchange up to three cards. (If a player has an Ace, he can trade in the other four cards in his hand.) The dealer deals new cards if needed so that every player always has a total of five. Another round of betting follows. Then it's time for the showdown, where everyone shows his cards and the person with the best hand wins.

The game continues until one player has all the chips and is declared the winner.

Standard variations:

WILD CARDS: Add wild cards to play.

HIGH/LOW: The highest hand and lowest hand split the pot.

LOWBALL: Lowest hand wins.

DOUBLE DRAW: After the first exchange and subsequent betting, there is another round of exchange and betting.

seven card stud

This classic poker game allows for many rounds of betting, which is especially fun for kids.

What you need:

Standard deck of cards (Ace is high)

Tokens, such as chips or candy

2 or more players

Goal:

To have the highest five-card hand

How to play:

Players ante up. The dealer deals each player two cards face down and one card face up. Players look at the cards that were placed face down.

The player with the lowest card showing puts in a small bet; betting continues to the player's left. When the betting is complete, the dealer gives each player one more card, face up. Another round of betting takes place, this time beginning with the player who has the highest cards showing. (From this point on, the player with the highest cards showing bets first.) After this, a fifth card is dealt face up. Another round of betting follows, and then a sixth card is dealt face up. Again, a round of betting follows. The seventh card is dealt face down to the players who remain. After one final round of betting, everyone shows his hand. The player who can make the best five-card hand (from the seven cards he has), wins. Continue the game until one person has all the chips. She is the winner.

cooking for card sharks

You'll want to make bite-size goodies for kids who are trying to grasp a handful of cards and nibble at the same time. The first two recipes resemble traditional hot dogs and hamburgers, but with a fun twist. The third is a variation on the ever-popular kid's meal: chicken fingers. All are easy enough for the kids to make with minimal help from an adult. Add a communal plate of celery and carrot sticks to round out the meal.

TIP: For kids, it's often the name that counts. Would they eat celery with peanut butter and raisins if it wasn't called Ants on a Log? In addition to experimenting with new recipes, try re-naming tried-and-true dishes to see if you can generate some interest in mealtime.

ROADKILL BURGERS

Ingredients:

1 pound ground beef

1 ½ cups shredded cheddar cheese

1 6-ounce can French fried onions

2 cans crescent rolls

Brown ground beef; drain fat.

Mix cheese and onions into the ground beef.

Place a spoonful of the beef mixture onto a crescent roll and fold it over to seal in the filling. Repeat with rest of rolls and meat.

Place burgers on ungreased cookie sheet. Bake at 350 degrees for about 8 minutes or until light brown.

PIGGIES IN A BLANKET

Ingredients:

1 package of mini hot dogs

1 can crescent rolls

Unroll the dough and separate it along the perforations. Cut each dough triangle into thirds.

Roll each piece of dough around one mini hot dog. Repeat with remainder of dough.

Bake at 350 degrees on ungreased cookie sheet for about 12 minutes or until light brown.

(Serve with your favorite dipping sauce for the "piggies," like honey mustard.)

FOWL FINGERS

Ingredients:

1 6-ounce can French fried onions

¼ cup flour

2 pounds boneless chicken tenders

2 large eggs, beaten

Put the fried onions and flour together in a large, re-sealable plastic bag.

With a rolling pin, crush the fried onions inside the bag. Dump the contents onto a plate.

Dip the chicken pieces into the beaten egg, then coat in the onion and flour mixture.

Bake at 400 degrees for 15 minutes.

(Serve with fun dipping sauces like honey mustard or spicy buffalo ranch.)

CHAPTER SIXTEEN

ideas for a family talent show night

If you're ready for a new kind of Family Fun Night, try spending an evening showing off your talents (or lack of talent)! Chuck Barris's The Gong Show from the 1970s (and more recently, American Idol auditions) have proven that it can be as entertaining to watch people without talent as it is to watch gifted people perform. Depending on the range of ability in your group, you can focus on the talent, lack of talent, or combine both for an evening of unique and unforgettable entertainment!

If you are a gifted singer or acrobat, then you need no suggestions for a talent show act. If, however, you're like most of us who can barely hit the notes of the Happy Birthday Song and couldn't do a somersault (even downhill), then you'll appreciate this list of 20 ideas for talent show acts that require little or no actual talent.

TIP: Don't overlook legitimate (though often unsung) talents within the family! Can your daughter show off her karate moves or twirl a basketball on the tip of her finger? Can your son do yoyo tricks? Can Dad whistle just about anything? Can Mom make amazing shadow puppets? You may have a talented family and not even realize it!

1. Read poetry aloud.

For serious selections, check out Caroline Kennedy's *A Family of Poems: My Favorite Poetry for Children*. For something sillier, try one of Shel Silverstein's wonderful books of poetry.

2. Sing a duet...with yourself!

Dress and make up your left side as a man and your right side as a woman. Lip-sync a song with both a female and a male part. Turn your profile to one side or the other, depending on which voice is singing.

3. Play the kazoo.

Any song will do.

4. Perform a skit with chin faces.

Any act delivered by "chin faces" is sure to be outrageously funny! To prepare, actors lie on their backs (ideally on a large ottoman) so that their heads are upside down. The designated make-up person draws eyes and a nose on each actor's chin and then gently covers the rest of his face so that only the chin and mouth are visible. Then, let the play begin! Actors won't be able to read anything because their eyes will be covered, but they can deliver a pre-rehearsed performance or they can improvise!

5. Juggle scarves.

They float, so even if you've never juggled anything in your life, you'll be able to juggle scarves.

6. Bring Fido into the act.

Show off some tricks you've taught the family pet. (Or come up with your own "tricks" that require the animal to do nothing other than be itself!)

7. Perform a comedy routine.

Get some joke books from the library or go online to find great material. Visit http://kids.yahoo.com/jokes for comedic inspiration!

TIP: Need more ideas? Check out www.talentedvideos.com and watch the crazy things other people have done!

8. Do impressions...

...of each other, the neighbors, the school crossing guard, Uncle Charlie, or even the family pet! Use props and costumes. Make the audience guess who you're imitating, turning your act into a combination of charades and impersonations!

9. Do the Chicken Dance.

(Check out a YouTube version to refresh your memory.)

10. Be Bill Nye the Science Guy.

Check out a few websites (like www.nyelabs.com or www.easy-kids-science-experiments.com) and wow everyone with your amazing scientific tests and experiments!

11. Hop, skip, and jump.

Practice jump rope tricks and then show off the best ones to the family.

12. Play The Question Game with a partner.

No need to rehearse for this performance; it's best as an impromptu act. The simple premise is that the entire conversation must consist of questions. Keep going until someone can't come up with a logical question and then start a different conversation, or pull someone else on "stage" to play.

13. "Clink out" a song.

Fill glasses with various levels of water and play a song by tapping them with a spoon.

14. Copy a popular camp routine.

One person stands in front of the other with his hands behind his back. The person in the back slips her arms through the sleeves of the one in front so that it appears that her arms are actually his. Then they act out a previously agreed-upon skit. (Acts involving eating and drinking, putting on make-up, and gesturing are particularly funny!)

15. Perform a little magic.

Practice a few card and magic tricks and show off your newfound skills to the rest of the family. Watch YouTube videos or visit how-to sites for ideas.

TIP: Play an instrumental CD in the background when non-musical acts, like yoyo stunts or magic tricks, are "on stage."

16. Have a shadow play.

Hang a plain sheet in a double doorway or string it across a corner of the room. Place a spotlight or other strong light bulb about 8 feet behind the curtain so that the beam of light is aimed at the sheet. Turn off all other lights in the room. Actors must stand behind and close to the sheet to create the best shadow. Music can accompany the play, a narrator can read lines, or the actors themselves can speak.

 MY STORY

"My kids put on a shadow play for us that involved a patient complaining of a stomach ache while a doctor extracted all sorts of items from the patient's stomach and discussed each one. It was so funny because the items he pulled out included things like a French horn, a spatula, and a dog's leash!"

-Nina, mother of four

17. Make a peanut butter and jelly sandwich...

...with instructions from your kids. Have your kids tell you step-by-step how to make the sandwich and do exactly what they say. If someone says, "Put peanut butter on the bread," take the entire jar and set it on top of the loaf of bread!

MY STORY

"We got my daughter a karaoke machine for her birthday and we love to set it up and sing karaoke as a family! We don't care what we sound like, we just have fun!"

-Juanita, mother of two

18. Hoop it up.

Revisit the '60s by showing off some hula-hoop tricks. Check out www.hooping.org for ideas.

19. Do a little improv acting.

Divide the family into two teams and give each a paper bag filled with assorted (random) objects like a banana, a flashlight, a spoon, a sock, and a stapler. Teams have five minutes to discuss what kind of a play they will perform using all of the objects in the bag.

20. Put on a puppet show.

A spring-tension rod suspended in a doorframe can support a curtain that will hide the puppeteers. Little puppeteers can use an appliance box with an opening cut out so that the puppets can peak out. You can create simple puppets with paper bags, socks, or even your fists!

TIP: Be sure to videotape your performance so that you can enjoy it in the years to come!

the _____ family
talent show

Location: _____

Date: _____

Time: _____

Starring: _____

_____

_____

Act 1: _____

_____

Act 2: _____

_____

Intermission

Act 3: _____

_____

Act 4: _____

_____

Curtain call

CHAPTER SEVENTEEN

family scavenger hunt night

If you're looking for a unique way to bond as a family, embark on a family scavenger hunt! Scavenger hunts have been popular with kids and adults for generations. Today's hunts are much more varied than the ones you might remember participating in as a Boy Scout or at a birthday party years ago. From Internet hunts that don't require participants to leave the living room to spooky graveyard adventures, scavenger hunts can take a variety of forms, and they can be tailored to fit any number of themes, occasions, or locations. Hunts foster teamwork and cooperation among siblings and require them to use their creative problem-solving skills.

When you organize your hunt, decide what your goal is, other than family bonding. Do you want your kids to become familiar with a certain area of town? Do you want to have an entertaining video of the event to watch later? Do you want the kids to learn something new?

Determine how participants will prove what they've seen or done (unless the hunt requires collecting specific items). You may ask for signatures, photos, or information filled out on a sheet of paper.

Create a list of items to be "scavenged." Decide if different items have different point values and assign those. Is a signature from Mr. Brown, the cranky neighbor no one ever sees, worth more than a signature from Mrs. Jones, who is warm and friendly and will inevitably offer visitors a slice of pie?

Finally, you may want to do a test run of the hunt to make sure that it is practical and feasible. You can tweak the list if some items seem like they will be too hard (or easy) to find.

MY STORY

"We let each of our kids invite one friend when we do family scavenger hunts, and then my husband and I each take two kids around. It's more fun for them and we love to watch them brainstorm with their buddy as they try to find the next item. It's loads of fun."

-Joanie, mother of two

There are as many different kinds of scavenger hunts as there are people to conceive them. You are limited only by your imagination (and the level of embarrassment your kids are willing to endure!). Listed here are some of the more popular, as well as a few unique, hunts for families.

mall hunt

A shopping mall hunt is especially fun if your kids are pre-teens or teens and are old enough to explore the mall on their own. If you live in an area without a mall, a safe, compact downtown area can work just as well. It's best to have a time limit, as kids can get distracted easily in stores. There are several variations on the Mall Hunt theme:

➡ Organize a traditional Mall Hunt, requiring each team to get the items on a list you've created, such as: a penny found face-up, a compliment from a store clerk, a packet of sugar with the name of a restaurant on it, something that costs less than 25 cents, a brochure for a fun activity in the area, a shopping bag that has red letters on it, or an old receipt for another person's purchase.

➡ Give teams a list of clues that will lead them to particular stores. In each store, they will need to get certain things, such as the price of a particular item or a credit card application. If you have the time, you can go to the stores ahead of time and ask the store managers to hand your kids the clue that will take them to the next location. (One group should start at one end of the mall while the other group starts at the opposite end. This way the teams are not following each other from store to store.)

➡ Rather than items to find, you can have the teams complete certain tasks like whistling an entire song in the middle of a jewelry store, trying on a tuxedo or a tiara, saluting a store employee, stretching out on a mall bench, asking a fellow shopper a question in a crazy accent, or sampling something in the food court. You should give each team a digital camera to record the events. Team members can print out the photos at a drugstore as the final step in the hunt.

➡ Give each team five dollars. How many different items can each team purchase with its money? (No fair buying 500 gumballs!) Set a time limit and a place to meet when the hunt is over.

TIP: Be sure everyone has a charged cell phone that is turned on so that you can keep track of the group as they explore the mall.

neighborhood hunt

If you know the neighbors well (or want to get to know them better!), send your family on a hunt in the neighborhood. Two groups can go door-to-door collecting items on a list such as a take-out menu, a used dryer sheet, or a dandelion from a neighbor's weedy lawn. You'll want to let the neighbors know ahead of time that your kids will be stopping by as part of a game. Set a time limit to keep the groups moving right along (and let them know that in the event that both teams are able to get everything on their lists, the team returning home first is the winner). Each team should have the same list of items, but it's best to have them ask for different things from different people.

photo or video hunt

Rather than check items off a list, your scavenger hunt teams can take photos of specific things. Each team can head out with a camera and a list as well as instructions for a meeting time and place. In a mall, for example, you could ask teams to photograph things like a mannequin with short black hair, a person pushing two kids in a stroller, or people holding hands. You can decide whether one or more team members must be included in each photo.

TIP: For even more outrageous fun, you can mandate that a certain object (a favorite stuffed animal, for example) must be included in every photograph!

In an interesting twist on the Photo Hunt idea, you take photos ahead of time of landmarks, signs, statues and other items within walking distance of your house or downtown. Then crop the photos so that only a portion shows. Each team is given a printout of all of the photos and is asked to identify every object within a set period of time. You could photograph the last few letters of graffiti on a building, a unique door or door handle, a parking meter that leans to one side, a brightly painted fire hydrant, and other similarly distinctive objects.

You could also plan a hunt using video, rather than still, cameras. You'll need two video cameras, one for each team, as well as a list of actions and situations each team is required to capture on tape. Team members might be asked to film themselves doing certain things (like helping someone to the car with her groceries or holding an elevator for someone who is trying to get on) or videotape specific situations involving other people (a little child jumping over puddles). The situations can require teams to perform helpful acts around town or do silly or challenging things. Each video segment shouldn't run longer than a minute or so to make later viewing easy.

 # MY STORY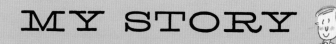

"When my kids and I tried a photo scavenger hunt, I was nervous about letting them use my digital camera. Instead, they took pictures with their cell phones and uploaded them onto our computer when the hunt was over! It was so easy, the kids had a great time, and I didn't have to worry about my expensive camera being damaged or lost!"

-Jonas, father of two

information hunt

Instead of looking for items on a list, teams embarking on an Information Hunt (armed with a list as well as a map) are looking for specific knowledge. Teams might be asked to find the date on the cornerstone of a building, figure out the phone number of the only remaining pay phone in town, find out what it costs to buy a cup of coffee at a certain restaurant, record the date on a particular tombstone, or other data of interest in your town. The team with the most correct answers within a certain time frame wins.

treasure hunt

A treasure hunt is a specific type of scavenger hunt in which a series of clues lead to a final "treasure." One clue leads to the next until the end of the hunt. A clue may be in the form of a riddle or may give directions (walk ten paces and turn left, for instance). A treasure hunt requires someone to set out clues ahead of time in places where they won't be disturbed, like underneath a park bench. Teams compete to see which one will be the first to solve the clues and get to the treasure. You can also have family members work together to reach the final destination where the treasure awaits. The "treasure" can be an object like a movie the family has been wanting to see or a destination like a favorite family restaurant where you'll then have dinner.

 MY STORY

"We hide treasure hunt clues in plastic Easter eggs so that the kids will recognize them. We also make sure they are in places where someone else isn't likely to pick them up and take them!"

-Caryn, mother of three

graveyard hunt

A Graveyard Hunt is perfect for a Family Fun Night that is close to Halloween and can be done in teams or individually, as you'll all be within a confined area. Create a list of a dozen or so items for everyone to find. (This may require you to visit the cemetery ahead of time to make sure that the items you've listed can be located there.) Rather than having players check items off of a list, provide everyone with paper and crayons or pencils so that they can create rubbings of each item they discover.

Your list can include items like a tombstone with a picture of an animal on it, an epitaph that includes the word "love," a tombstone with someone named "John" on it, a tombstone that lists a birth date that matches someone in the family, or a tombstone that is exactly 100 years old. You can award extra points to the team or person who finds the oldest tombstone, the deceased who lived the longest or the shortest life, the deceased with the longest first or last name, or the tombstone with the most names on it.

sound hunt

Scavenger hunters can listen for, rather than look for, items on a list, and record them on a tape recorder (or on a cell phone that can record sounds). The kinds of sounds you can include on a list are a bell ringing, a dog barking, a certain advertisement on the radio, or a train whistle. Certain sounds may be worth more points than others, depending on the likelihood that the players will hear them. You may want to define the area where teams are permitted to go and set an end time. Award the win to the team who records the greatest number of sounds from the list.

around the house hunt

The classic scavenger hunt involves searching for designated items around the house or in the backyard and returning within a certain amount of time. The simplest hunt to organize, the Around the House Hunt can require participants to find things as simple as a blue toy, or as tricky as something that doesn't belong in the house or something that is missing a part. You can get silly (requiring people to find sporks or light sabers) or practical (a postage stamp or a ten-year-old penny).

"We organize a scavenger hunt during the winter that the kids just love. Ahead of time, we make colored ice cubes: lots of blue and green ones and just a few reds (they are worth the most points). Then we hide them outside and the kids run around and try to find them. They forget that it's 20 degrees out there!"

-Jeffrey, father of four

missing pieces hunt

Your family can work as a team to find the missing pieces of a puzzle or object that you've hidden ahead of time. Hiding them in your house or yard is the easiest and most convenient thing to do, although you can take this hunt to a public area if you're sure other people won't disturb the objects. You can use pieces of a jigsaw puzzle or you can connect this hunt to a theme by, for example, taking apart a plastic jointed skeleton and hiding its pieces for Halloween.

TIP: To make a pre-arranged hunt even more fun, have it at night and hide items that glow in the dark. You can make items shine by applying glow-in-the-dark paint (available online) which, when applied to most surfaces, will create a glow that lasts for more than 20 hours.

people hunt

Have your family scavenger hunters search for people rather than things! You could include people you know or complete strangers. As proof that they located the people on the list, players could collect autographs or business cards. The list could include someone named Bill, someone who has at least four children, someone who is or used to be a teacher, someone who looks like a celebrity, and so on. A parent will want to accompany each team for safety reasons.

TIP: You can combine various elements from different hunts to create a truly unique experience. You might include things to photograph, things to collect, information to uncover, and clues to solve.

internet hunt

An Internet hunt is perfect when it's inconvenient to leave home, or when you want to play with someone remotely, such as family members in college. All that's needed is a computer with Internet access for each player. These hunts are often used as a learning tool for students who need to know how to search the Internet. Compile a list of things your hunters will look for or information they need to find; the fastest one to finish wins. (As an added bonus, this is great practice for kids who need to look things up for homework.)

TIP: Make sure you monitor the Internet searches of your younger kids so that they don't stumble across any inappropriate content online.

TIDBIT: Rick Gates, a library science student, created the first Internet Scavenger Hunt in 1992. He wanted to urge people to explore the many resources on the Internet. He distributed questions through a variety of sites and offered a prize to those who completed the hunt.

alphabet hunt

After you've agreed on a theme and location for the hunt, each team heads out with a list lettered from A to Z. In the pre-determined time, each team must find one item that begins with each letter. The hunt can take place in your neighborhood, on a playground, in a shopping mall, or in your own house.

 ## MY STORY

"We like to do a Holiday Hunt around Christmas time. My wife and I each drive a couple of kids around town looking for things like an inflatable snowman on someone's lawn, a tree covered in only blue lights, a nativity scene… that type of thing. Whichever team finds everything on the list first wins!"

-Tim, father of four

math hunt

Put your arithmetic skills to good use in this Math Hunt! This is an easy contest to judge: The team that returns home with the correct answer wins! No need for a team to check items off lists, take photos, or offer anything else as proof of its accomplishments!

This will require a little prep work on your part. You'll need to drive around town (or the designated area for the hunt) and develop a list of questions that relate to familiar landmarks and locations. Then you can create a simple math problem to represent each question. When all of the math problems are worked out in order, you'll have a numerical answer. That's all each team needs to bring home at the end of the hunt!

For example:

The number of mailboxes directly outside the post office

X

The number of gas pumps at the convenience store on the corner

+

The number of windows on the front of the elementary school

—

The number of parking spots in front of the print shop

...and so on. Work out about a dozen problems and then calculate the answer. Double-check your answer. The first team to return home with the right answer wins! (If the first ones back don't have the correct answer, they can head out and try again.)

our family's
scavenger hunt

Name of hunt: _____

Location(s): _____

_____

_____

Time limit, if any: _____

Special instructions: _____

_____

_____

_____

_____

_____

_____

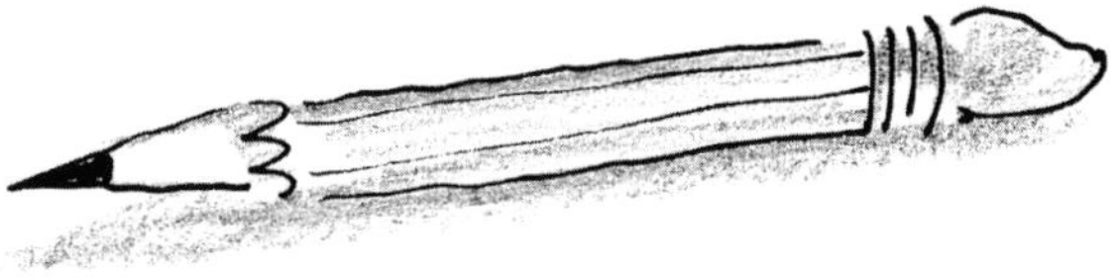

Items needed (with point values, if appropriate):

❑ _____

❑ _____

❑ _____

❑ _____

❑ _____

❑ _____

❑ _____

❑ _____

❑ _____

❑ _____

❑ _____

❑ _____

❑ _____

❑ _____

❑ _____

❑ _____

❑ _____

❑ _____

❑ _____

family memories night

"We do not remember days…
we remember moments."

-Cesare Pavese

Some family evenings are for creating new memories and some are for remembering wonderful times from the past. Nothing brings a family closer than recalling and celebrating the shared experiences that are part of a family's journey. Whether you decide to watch old home movies or turn vacation photos into placemats or pillowcases, take an evening to stroll, skip, or dash down memory lane with your kids.

show slides at a family "drive-in"

Hang a white sheet on the side of your house. Run an extension cord and set up the slide projector so that you can show slides outside. If younger kids get bored now and then, they can dash around the yard. If soda spills… So what? That's the beauty of being outside!

TIP: Make sure you transfer home movies from videotape to DVD. After a number of years, tapes begin to deteriorate. Many online services will convert your VHS tapes for $15 to $20 per tape. You can also ask for price information at the film counter of your local drug store.

make a funniest-thing-that-ever-happened book

Start a family notebook for funny memories. You can spend a Family Fun Night decorating the cover with a collage of photographs and words cut out of magazines. Keep it in a central location and when something funny happens, whether it's a little sibling saying "babing suit" or someone forgetting to add sugar to the pumpkin pie at Thanksgiving, write it down. Every year on New Year's Eve, read all of the entries from the previous 12 months.

 MY STORY

"We have a family notebook in which I've written prompts at the top of every page like "My favorite thing to do with dad is…" and "I wish that I could …" Some are serious and some are silly. Once a week, each child fills in one page of his choosing. The results are truly priceless."

-Eva, mother of three

make placemats with vacation memorabilia

Remind your kids about all of the fun they've had on family vacations by making 11" x 17" collages out of photographs, ticket stubs, brochures, restaurant napkins—anything and everything you saved from the trip. The kids can even draw pictures of things they remember. Photocopy and laminate each one at an office supply store to create lasting placemats as reminders of family fun.

 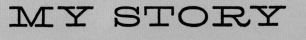

MY STORY

"Whenever we do family craft projects, I organize supplies and do a lot of the prep work ahead of time. I find that if everything is ready to go when the kids sit down at the table, they're more likely to stick with the project until it's done."

-Carmen, mother of three

make a family time capsule

Preserve some family memories in a time capsule! You can purchase a time capsule that will last for many generations or simply put items in a plastic storage bin and tuck it up on a shelf for a designated number of years. Add things like family photos, a favorite recipe, a t-shirt from a race or event, pages from the newspaper, a wrapper from your favorite food, drawings or letters—anything that represents your family or the year that you are putting things away. It's especially meaningful for everyone to write a letter to his or her future self. As each person puts at item into the time capsule, he can explain the importance of it and why he wants to preserve it.

 MY STORY

"We took photos of meaningful items that were just too large to put in our time capsule. In one photo, my son is holding up this paper mache robot he made for art class that is wearing glasses just like his."

-Connie, mother of two

MY STORY

"Just before she graduated from high school, my daughter opened a time capsule that she had put together in first grade. She had a wonderful time looking at everything she'd saved, and she actually used the letter she wrote back then as inspiration for a speech she delivered at her graduation."

-Cindy, mother of three

videotape an older relative telling stories

Spend an evening with grandparents or other older relatives and videotape them recalling tales of their youth. Kids should arrive with questions to prompt them like, "What's the funniest thing you remember your father doing?" or "What's the most trouble you got into when you were young?" Later, you can edit the tapes using a video-editing program like iMovie on your computer.

write funny captions for family photos

Enlarge a particularly funny or unique photo of each member of the family and draw enough speech bubbles so that each person can write a "quote." You can put them in a scrapbook or turn them into placemats (see earlier entry).

 MY STORY

"There are great craft kits available in craft supply stores or from catalogs like Hearthsong. If you want to make family crafts as stress-free as possible, use kits rather than trying to pull together all of the supplies yourself."

-Louise, mother of four

set aside an evening for storytelling

Storytelling is a lost art, but you can help revive it. Talk to your kids about things you remember from your own childhood, from when they were younger, or just interesting tales that you want to share. Experts advise that you tell stories that you love in your own style and voice that have a clear beginning, middle, and end. Speak more slowly and louder than you think you need to, using gestures that feel natural.

share your memories with loved ones

Share photos with your extended family and far-away friends by creating an online photo album using a site like www.shutterfly.com or www.flickr.com. Just email the link to your album and others can enjoy the photos from your last vacation—or your last Family Fun Night! (Not all photo-sharing sites are free, so be sure to read the fine print.)

put your mug on a mug!

Upload your digital pictures to www.snapfish.com to create one-of-a-kind mugs, photo books, pillowcases, cards, calendars, key chains, or even mouse pads! It's easy to do and relatively inexpensive.

create scrapbook pages

Keep scrapbooking supplies (scissors, glue sticks, thin makers, stickers, stamps…) in a special box and let each child design his own page. Make copies of photos so that kids can cut, crop, and trim as much as they want to. Put all the pages together when you're done for a truly memorable scrapbook.

make stepping-stones

Using a mix like Quikrete, follow the instructions to create concrete. Scoop the concrete into old pie plates, smoothing the top with a scrap of wood. Wait about an hour and a half, then let every member of the family customize one stone with beach glass, shells, pebbles, and other small weather-proof items. Cover each stone with a dishcloth and spray each with water a few times every day to cure them. In a few days, they will be ready to set outside.

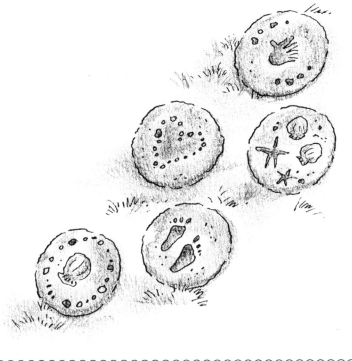

my favorite family memory is...

Name: _____ Age: _____

My favorite family memory is: _____

_____

_____

_____

Name: _____ Age: _____

My favorite family memory is: _____

_____

_____

_____

Name: _____ Age: _____

My favorite family memory is: _____

_____

_____

_____

Name: _____ Age: _____

My favorite family memory is: _____

_____

_____

_____

Name: _____ Age: _____

My favorite family memory is: _____

_____

_____

_____

Name: _____ Age: _____

My favorite family memory is: _____

_____

_____

_____

Name: _____ Age: _____

My favorite family memory is: _____

_____

about the author

Cynthia L. Copeland is the best-selling and award-winning author of over 25 books for parents and children. Her work has been featured on Good Morning America, selected for Oprah's "O List" in *O Magazine*, recommended by Ann Landers, and featured in *Family Circle* Magazine. Copeland has sold over three-quarters of a million books in at least five languages. She currently lives in New Hampshire with her husband and three children.

needs glasses but pretends she doesn't

talks too fast because she is easily excited

lives in sweatshirts and pajama pants

always has a messy desk

has hair that is too long for someone her age (but is trusting best friend Mary Brett to tell her kindly when it's time to get it cut)

has 2 holes in each ear because teenage daughter talked her into it

is afraid of new computer

Cynthia L. Copeland (call her "Cindy")

about cider mill press

Good ideas ripen with time. From seed to harvest, Cider Mill Press strives to bring fine reading, information, and entertainment together between the covers of its creatively crafted books. Our Cider Mill bears fruit twice a year, publishing a new crop of titles each spring and fall.

CIDER MILL
PRESS

BOOK
PUBLISHERS
Where good books
are ready for press

**Visit us on the web at:
www.cidermillpress.com**

**Or write to us at:
12 Port Farm Road
Kennebunkport, Maine 04046**